EDGE OF DARKNESS, EDGE OF LIGHT

R. S. Scriven is the author of more than thirty radio plays, and the following published works:

A SINGLE TAPER and THE INWARD EYE: BOY 1913, The Partridge Press, 1953

THE YEAR OF THE PHOENIX AND OTHER POEMS, Secker & Warburg in association with The Partridge Press, 1959

THE PROSPECT OF WHITBY, illustrated by Doreen Robert, Oxford University Press, 1971

THE THINGUMMY JIG, Penguin Education, 1973

THE POLTER GOOSE, Penguin Education, 1973

THE FAIRY TALE COOK BOOK, Eurobooks, 1974

THE SEASONS OF THE BLIND and other Radio Plays in Verse, British Broadcasting Corporation, 1974

EDGE OF DARKNESS, EDGE OF LIGHT

by

R.C. SCRIVEN

SOUVENIR PRESS

CONTENTS

ACKNOWLEDGMENTS

I am rich and in debt, for I owe a world of thanks to a world of friends. Colleagues, editors, sound radio producers, actors, actresses and technicians — they will, I know, smile away my embarrassment over not mentioning anyone individually.

I am grateful to each and every one of them.

The author would like to thank Messrs Duckworth & Co for permission to quote from the poem DEDICATORY ODE by Hilaire Belloc; the Society of Authors as the literary representatives of the Estate of A. E. Housman, and Jonathan Cape Ltd, publishers of A. E. Housman's *Collected Poems*, for permission to quote lines from A. E. Housman; the Society of Authors as the literary representatives of the Estate of John Masefield for permission to quote from BEAUTY; M. B. Yeats, Miss Ann Yeats and the Macmillan Co. of London and Basingstoke for permission to quote from THE SONG OF WANDERING AENGU from *The Collected Poems* of W. B. Yeats; and Peter Newbolt for permission to quote from *Drake's Drum* and *Vitaï Lampada* by Henry Newbolt. The lines from THE CONGO by Vachel Lindsay are reprinted with permission of MacMillan Publishing Co. Inc. from *Collected Poems* of Vachel Lindsay; copyright 1914 by Macmillan Publishing Co. Inc., renewed 1942 by Elizabeth C. Lindsay.

Chapter 1

DECLINE AND RISE

Adam fell for an apple.

The comic spirit later suggested that the troubles of his descendants sprang from the pear on the ground. How much nobler an image is that of Lucifer, Son of the Morning, falling headlong out of heaven.

But the ridiculous *is* sublime.

My own sense of the ridiculous has its origins in the grass roots of a lawn in Sholebrook Avenue, Leeds. There, my memory began.

I jumped from the top of a heap of lawn mowings.

I have no recollection whatsoever of climbing that green hill, now so far away in time.

The shock of my crash landing made me fall BUMP! on my head.

I howled. I yelled: "Smack grass, smack grass."

But why on earth, I've asked myself ever since, did that one fall, out of the hundreds of tumbles I must have had by the time I was two-and-a-half, did that one fall trigger off my memory?

Shortly after my tumble headlong into my world of

memory, I thought I knew who I was. Ronald Charles Scriven.

I knew where I lived.

I didn't know that the place where I lived was a house.

I did know it was home.

Home was where Mother was, and Mother was home. She was always there. Except at mysterious intervals when she wasn't.

There were other figures, baffling, who appeared and disappeared in that landscape of my childhood.

My father was there and then he wasn't, but never *there* as my mother was. All that the child that I was knew of him was that he loved me. I knew too that Gran, who also appeared and vanished, loved me too. I didn't know that Gran was my mother's mother any more than I knew that Grandpa was my father's father. Grandpa had hoisted me on to his knee after I'd jumped off the grass heap, slid me down his leg and jogged me up and down on his foot.

"Ride a cock horse to Banbury Cross."

In my memory, new minted in those first ten minutes of its existence, my grandfather lives, moves and has his being.

Memory tells me not what my grandfather looked like but what he was: kindness without its armour on. Hindsight, the buttress of memory, tells me what he was with his armour on.

Born in the first decade of Victoria's reign, he was off the mark by the time he was thirty. He established the Leeds Old Foundry in Jack Lane, Hunslet, the city's heavy engineering district. By the time I was born he had added its logical complement, a machine-tool shop much nearer the city centre, in York Street within easy access to the main line railway stations.

A Victorian of Victorians, benevolence and philanthropy were part of his make-up.

Benevolence and philanthropy, on his own terms. He paid his men what he and they considered good wages. If they turned out not to be good workmen or, worse, attempted to argue with him, he sacked them. Controlling machines and the men who made the machines came naturally to him.

His philanthropy he channelled through Freemasonry. He was a founder member of the Goderich Lodge. He had all the trimmings which went with what he considered that honour. Masonic jewels, aprons, worshipful masterhood, mystical ritual, the lot. Furthermore, like good wages, it paid.

Charles Scriven had five children. James, his first-born, in 1874. Sarah Ann, the first girl, two years later. My father, John Boyle Scriven, known as Jack, the middle son, in 1884. Jess, the second girl, and then Norman, the youngest and last boy.

My grandfather was and knew himself to be the driving force of his firm and his family. It was obvious to Charles that to shape their lives and give those lives purpose was in the best interests of his children.

But flesh and blood is intractable stuff. Children are by nature rebellious. James was rebellious. So his father tamed him. Sarah Ann, being a girl, was brought up and shaped by her mother. Everyone called her Ciss. My grandmother went about the bringing up in her own sweet way. Her husband did not notice what that way was. Why should he? He was under the agreeable illusion that he was as absolutely master in his house as he was in the foundry. He did not notice that the seeds of rebellion were in Ciss.

Latent, but there.

The period itself conditioned her to its maxim that children should be seen and not heard, especially on Sundays.

One of the most soothing aspects of my grandfather's agreeable illusion was that all the clocks in the house, and there were many, were kept accurate to five seconds either way of the time kept by his very expensive gold watch. His longcase grandfather clock, a Tompion, kept in tick with his watch week by week.

The winding of grandfather by my grandfather was as central a ritual in his life as the tyling of his Masonic lodge.

He noticed, how could he help noticing, that my grandmother's grandmother clock was blatantly out of both tick and tock with the rest.

He was a kindly, an indulgent man.

And after all nobody in the house took any notice of that clock save my grandmother herself.

From a very early age it became obvious that Jack had inherited his father's engineering abilities. His special flair was for draughtsmanship. He conformed gladly to his father's specifications for his future. He went into the firm's drawing office in his late teens and married Ruth Gertrude Briggs with his father's full approval soon after he came of age. The only shadow cast over the wedding feast was that of my mother. The entire family turned out on parade for that marriage, the first in my father's generation. The Victorian great aunts were for once of a like mind. Gertie was suspect. They felt it in their bones. And what the great aunts felt in their bones, all the other women in the family felt, apprehensively, in theirs.

Gertie was spirited. She was light-headed. She was a *New Woman*.

What was the New Woman? Well, she was a cloud no larger than Sylvia Pankhurst's head, threatening, not the nation's security, but its general peace of mind.

Suffragettes. Heaving half-bricks at policemen. Chaining themselves to the railings of Downing Street. Aping militancy as Flora Drummond led their marches on a white horse, disturbing, vexatious to the Victorians. Wonderful women. This girl Jack had married at St Clement's would, the great aunts darkly suspected, be heaving half-bricks as soon as the honeymoon was over, if not before.

James, whose social mind had set like concrete by the time he was twenty, must have seemed to the Old Guard a reassuring figure – and there was nineteen stones of him to add weight to that reassurance. None of them would live for ever, even though it had seemed Victoria would.

How I can now sympathise with their feelings. It was 1906.

Victoria's shadow, in the lifetime of all of them, had covered about three quarters of the globe. Her short, dumpy figure, lissome when she was a girl, had been the embodiment of the greatest power of a long epoch.

Only the younger lot, like Jack and Gertie, were looking forward eagerly to a future without her. If they looked over their shoulders, it was at the Naughty Nineties, anathema to their elders.

Hence the lightness of my mother's step, the confidence of my father's. For the whole country in the middle of the garden-party reign of Edward the Peacemaker was confident that the coming century would be the start of a thousand years of peace, progress and prosperity. Why, they told themselves, the Boer War would go down in history as the last of all wars.

By the time Jack returned from his honeymoon, my grandfather had his plans for his second son's future off the drawing board, blue-printed and ready to be machined. Jack was to go to Sheffield where he would set him up as a consulting engineer. The firm had plenty of associates in the greatest steel city in Europe. Some of them could be relied on to put business Jack's way, to assess his calibre and keep in with the firm. Scriven's had important business links with the great bridge-building firm of Dorman, Long of Middlesborough. They had an important branch in Sheffield. So had Babcock and Wilcox who made the famous Lancashire boilers. So had Charles Parsons of Newcastle. Jack would make his way.

He and Gertie were installed in a small, stone-built house at 12 Raven Road, in a spur of the hills, not far from the Derbyshire border. Aunt Jess told me that my father called it his Raven's Nest.

There, I was born, Sunday's child on the 21st of April 1907

Jack had done what was expected of him: begun, to the profit of the firm, to make his way.

Gertie had done all and more than all of a daughter-in-law's duty. She had produced me and by doing so assured the continuance of the line. Never again in my grandfather's hearing did even the most formidable great aunt dare to criticise Gertie for being a New Woman.

But if my grandfather rather lost his head over me, he kept it very coolly with his son. It would be in the best interests of Jack and therefore of the firm if he stayed where he was for a couple of years. After that, he'd be made a partner.

When this news reached James, he nerved himself to protest.

He got short shrift.

"Do as your brother has done. Marry and beget me another grandson and then we'll see."

James protested "But Father, I can't marry until I meet the right woman." "You've had more time than Jack to find her." "Marry on what?" blustered James, "I get my keep and a pound or two pocket money. Jack gets commission on top of a salary."

"And why not? He has the expense of a married man to meet, household bills, a wife to keep and now my grandson. I won't have you being jealous of your brother, James. Your turn will come."

That would put James on his mettle. My grandfather plumed himself. Things were turning out the way they should. On my second birthday he was as good as his word and whisked my father back to Leeds to be set up in Sholebrook Avenue and given his promised partnership.

Going from room to room of her new house, tinkling on her piano whenever she passed it, planking me on unopened packing cases, telling the men Jack had laid on from the works where to place a picture or a preserving pan and then changing her mind, mother was blissfully happy turning the carbolic smell of the house into the warm, flower-scented smell of home.

In our new home I trotted about at my father's heels to make the most of him while I could. More imitative than a barrel of monkeys, I began to copy the things he did. He still brought work home from the office. I'd about as much a notion of what work was as I had of what a drawing office was. I could see what he was doing though, drawing. So I drew, much better drawings. Daddy always drew the same thing. Lots of lines on paper. Sometimes black lines on white paper. Sometimes white lines on blue paper. They were the same old lines anyway. I drew all sorts of things. I liked drawing houses best. Houses were square. They had two windows and a door downstairs and two windows upstairs. They had a roof with a chimney pot. The drawing wasn't finished until I remembered to draw a wiggle which was the smoke coming out of the chimney pot.

"If you forget that," said Daddy, "The smoke will fill the kitchen and put the fire out, and you'll be black as the sweep." I liked that, so I tried to draw myself inside a house with no chimney pot but my crayons smudged and the house was black and I couldn't see me.

I was pleased by his looking at my drawings. I was cross that he wouldn't let me draw with the funny-looking pens he used. When he used them he stuck the tip of his tongue out of one corner of his mouth. I stuck the tip of my tongue out of the corner of mine. I didn't know I was doing this until Mother told me not to.

Why didn't she tell Daddy not to?

He brushed his teeth very hard and Mother told me to brush mine hard too.

Grandpa was sometimes there and sometimes not, but in quite a different way from Daddy. When Grandpa was there I didn't have to trot about after him. Grandpa kept me with him all the time. "He can't take his eyes off you," mother said.

There was a pool in the garden. I can see the shape of it now but not the size. The workmen, who called my grandfather Charles, just as he called each of the men by his Christian name, would have rubbed disbelieving eyes if they'd seen him folding sheets of *The Morning Post* into cocked-hat paper boats and then kneeling to launch them on the perilous sea of the pool. I would puff and he would huff and the floating cocked hat would set off, to founder midway, or veer at every strong puff of the wind if it chose to join in the game.

It was a game Grandpa and I with or without the wind could play the whole of a summer afternoon, which is as long as a week and as short as half a minute.

The thrilling part of the game was when a boat sailed right across and beached itself on the far shore. Grandpa would pace me to see who would reach it first. I always won. I loved Grandpa more and more every day.

I noticed all sorts of things about him. He wore a funny hat which sometimes fell into the pool. When it did, we both laughed until neither of us could draw another huff or puff.

One day, when the wind was a bit blowy and grandpa was folding another boat, I saw that he'd stuck the tip of his tongue out of the corner of his mouth.

When it rained, Grandpa played tiddlewinks with me on the dining room table.

Grandpa could read. I liked that, especially when the book had pictures in it. But better than being read to, I like the stories Grandpa told me. He knew ever so many things I didn't. I didn't know about Santa Claus. Grandpa said "He came last Christmas and he'll be coming down the chimney again this Christmas."

"When is Christmas, Grandpa?"

"Soon enough. I'll be coming along on Christmas morning to see what Santa's put in your stocking."

Soon enough was ages and ages.

One night Daddy and not Mummy put me to bed. "It's Christmas Eve," he said.

He hung up my stocking, it was one of Gran's really — ever so black and long and woolly. When he kissed me goodnight and God bless there was something the matter with his eyes, as if he was crying.

"I've got a speck of dust in them," he said.

I knew Daddy never cried. "God bless."

Santa did come. Lots and lots of presents. I was so excited that I didn't want my breakfast. It was a lovely, lovely day.

BANG BANG BANG and paper hats bursting out of crackers.

Daddy played with me and my new toys.

I wore my new blue dressing gown when Daddy gave me a piggyback to bed. It was only when he was tucking me in that I remembered something important.

"Daddy, why didn't Grandpa come to see what Santa Claus had put in my stocking? He promised he would."

"Yes," said Daddy, "I know."

I'd taken my new teddybear to bed with me. Daddy suddenly pressed the button in teddy's tummy and made him squeak.

"Grandpa will come when he can."

Charles Scriven had died on the 8th December. His death was to change the lives of all his family, for better, for worse, for richer, for poorer.

From beyond the grave that powerful instrument, his last will and testament, would control them wisely and guide them well.

Charles and his lawyers had foreseen and provided against every contingency they could jointly foresee. They had tied the will with the tightest of legal knots.

The will had been drawn up and signed not long after my birth, in full confidence that its provisions would be scrupulously carried into effect by his executors and I, his only grandson, would continue the rising fortunes of the family and the firm Charles Scriven had founded. I am confident he went to his fathers with mind and heart at ease when the fever of life was over, and he had found his rest and peace at the end.

I shall always be glad that I knew him as I did, kindly, loving and without his armour.

Chapter 2

A LITTLE RED BOX OF BRICKS

From beyond the grave the will of Charles Scriven continued to govern his firm and control the lives of his family.

But flesh and blood, poured into the mould of man, is a very different stuff than iron and steel.

To be master of his father's house, married to a wife who well suited him, James had returned soberly from his honeymoon. He took it for granted that his mother would be well pleased with the arrangements he and Florence had discussed and soon proposed to her.

"Everything will go on just as before, Mother. Florence will run the house for you. You can take things easy. You'll have your own quarters here and nothing whatever to worry about. Not even young Jess. We intend to look after her too, until she's through with her cookery course. Then she may either look after herself, stay on with us or what's much more likely, get married."

"My own quarters, James," said my grandmother, "in what was, for the whole of your life my own house?

No thank you."

James was astounded.

"I don't understand you, mother. It will still be your house."

"It is *not* my house any more. It's yours and Florence's."

"Then what do you want to do?" asked James. He looked at his wife for assistance. Florence said, "Do stay with us, we both want you."

"I want a small house of my own, somewhere near Harehills Avenue." Grandma sat down.

"If that's what you'd like, mother, why not go and live with Jack? Though I'm hanged if I see why you don't want to fall in with our suggestions."

"Of course I'm not going to live with Jack and Gertie. Even if I wanted to, they've got Gertie's mother living with them, not to mention Ronald to bring up. And there's another child on the way."

"Harrumph," said James.

"Don't you 'Harrumph' me, James. Arrange to buy me a nice little house which I can manage comfortably — nearby — so I can keep in touch with both you and Jack."

James, much put about, put himself about and having vetted the property, bought No 3, Ellers Road.

The house was a little red box-of-bricks in a quiet backwater off the residential stream of Harehills Avenue.

"Take whatever furniture from Francis Street you like to choose, mother. This is a miserable business."

In that big quietly rich old house, silver and gleam when linen was laid and never a draught had stirred the great dull crimson drapes, Grandma knew the furniture was too massive to take. Carpets, curtains, bed linen were on too ample a scale for the little house.

"There's nothing I really want, James. I'll take my matched pair of lustres your father bought me. My own grandmother clock. Now let me see. I couldn't get my concert grand piano into the new parlour and besides, Florence is a very talented pianist."

James shifted uneasily. He was not one to analyse shades of irony. Particularly women's.

"So I'd like a new small upright piano, a Bluthner."

James winced. Never mean, he was always careful in money matters. Particularly now, when the money happened to be not his own but his mother's. And he could foresee many other expenses.

He said "Very well. Very well. Anything else?"

"Jess, of course, will come with me. She may bring anything she likes from her own room. Her bed's about the only thing in Francis Street that isn't too big for Ellers Road."

So, grumpily, James arranged his mother's move and on the mantelshelf of her new bedroom, Jess arranged her own girlish momentoes. An autographed photo of Ellen Terry, a cheerfully ugly pottery model of G. E. Studdy's pup, Bonzo, and her small library.

Jess was the only member of the family left at home. Ciss had married a doctor, Harold Radcliffe, and was living in the country at South Milford.

Grandma Scriven's little red box-of-bricks enchanted me. When I was taken round to see her, she held me at arm's length. "What a big boy you've grown. Are you thirsty, Ronald? Give him some ginger beer, Jess."

Harry Holgate's stone ginger beer was sold in two-gallon brown earthenware bottles with a broad handle. When the wire was cut the flat cork went POP! The ginger beer gurgled and glugged into tumblers. Vanished from this wicked world I know where that ginger beer has gone. When the cherubs are loosed from practising alleluias, they rush to the free-for-all tuck shop just round the corner. St Nicholas benignly controls the free-for-all as the cherubs jostle and cheat as they queue for crystal goblets of Harry Holgate's ginger beer.

In Ellers Road, I drank and drank the paradisial stuff. The bubbles prickling and going popple, popple, popple in my nose.

"That boy's going to burst," Aunt Jess laughed. "I know he is."

She knew something else as well. Something I didn't.

Resigned to her widowhood, my grandmother had made up her mind to keep herself occupied. Like most good Victorian women, she believed that homemade wines were as wholesome as they were non-intoxicating. Inebriated by this belief she had resolved to make some.

She coveted Harry Holgate's stone bottles for the job. The more Jess topped me up the sooner my grandmother could set about bottling her wines. Great stone jars already filled with queer smelling brews were squatting in corners of her pantry.

A fortnight after my grandmother had been installed, James came gallumphing down from Francis Street to see how she was settling in. "Very nicely, James, thank you. Except for the mice and the draughts."

"Mice?" said James. "What mice?"

"They always come in from next door."

"That's what our next door neighbours say," said Jess giggling.

"Eh? Nonsense. Draughts? There isn't a draught in the house. I went over it thoroughly before I committed myself to buying the place. Jess, fetch a candle."

He went round every door, every window frame, every skirting board.

"You see, mother? Not a flicker."

"There is when the wind's in the wrong quarter."

"Humph," said James.

"And another thing, I don't like the colour of the front door."

"What's the matter with that? It's the same as all the other front doors in Ellers Road."

It was. They'd all been painted that favourite shade, dog-shit brown. It was thought to harmonise with that other affront to the eyesight, window frames painted a bilious green.

My grandmother had her own sweet way. Doors and windows were repainted to her fancy.

When I was born, the world was born. It took me a long time to discover that it was called Sholebroke Avenue. Then I found out that it wasn't called that any more, but Harehills Avenue.

When I got used to where the world was, it began to expand at a quite alarming rate. Its known boundaries were pushed as far as Miss Beal's Kindergarten, where I discovered there were so many, many more people in the world.

I found out that beyond the world's edges there were other worlds. The Olympia world, where Daddy and Mummy whizzed round and round on roller skates, going faster and faster among hundreds and hundreds of people.

Was Olympia the end of everywhere? And just as I had begun to find my bearings and knew, roughly, in which direction Olympia was and the way we went to Francis Street, my grandmother's little red box-of-bricks added an entirely new dimension to my world close at hand.

It wasn't only the ever-flowing fountain of Harry Holgate's ginger beer which made my grandmother's house so attractive. The going there was so exciting. I was taken there by so many different ways. One way was to go to church first, which I didn't like except that it meant that I could walk between Mummy and Daddy. Church was next door to my kindergarten but wasn't a bit like it. Then Ellers Road was just across the Avenue. Mummy took me there ever so many different ways. Soon I could recognise some of them. It was lovely going shopping on The Parade. Gosney's was a sweet shop which gave Daddy tobacco when he took me there, but gave me sweets when Mummy did. Paradise Fruits fizzed with sherbert when I sucked them long enough. I could suck everlasting toffee a lot longer but Mummy said it was nasty and made out of horse glue. She told Mr. Gosney to give me only dolly mixtures or dewdrops or Japs. Mummy never stayed long enough in Gosney's but she spent ages looking into the windows of *all* the shops on The Parade and popping in and out of them.

The Parade was a splendid way of going to Ellers Road.

You could get there by way of Hilltop Crescent, or by way of Potternewton Park which had a big house called a mansion, full of some birds called stuffed owls in glass cages. When I thought I knew all the ways of getting to Grandma's house, Mother surprised me by finding a new way from the far end of The Parade.

Guess what it turned out to be? The other end of Ellers Road and I was so pleased when I recognised Number 3 that I jigged up and down on the pavement.

These explorations showed me so many marvels that the wonder was I got them into my head. My mind was expanding faster than my ability to recognise how one part of my small world was related to another. I had only the sketchiest notions of scale and proportion. Wherever I happened to be was so intensely *there* that it absorbed my whole attention.

The Paradise Fruits in their big glass jars, the dolly mixtures in small triangular paper bags, were the focus of the immediate here and now. In Olympia, the hugeness of the place impressed me.

While I was exploring that minute part of it which was all the world to me, Edwardian England went into court mourning. The reign which my father thought was to usher in a thousand years of peace had ended.

Business, as usual, turned whatever it could lay its hand on into profit. Doggerel birds, their ears attuned to the mood of the people, rushed to the jobbing printers with broadsheets lamenting the death of the king: "He was our Dad. Saved the country one million."

What? The country was going to the dogs already: to the damnation bow-wows. Or so the pessimists said. Never mind. The British Empire was still the greatest the world had ever known. Put out more flags. Nothing like a coronation to cheer everybody up.

While all these events were happening, I was less concerned than a flower is by the day-to-day weather. Is the sky clouded? A dandelion still knows where the sun is. The leaves of all flowers open their hands to catch the longed for rain. Your countryman can tell what o'clock it is by the opening of the daisy's tight-clenched fist, the closing of the shepherd's purse.

I'd tried to write before I could read and got into paddywhacks because grownups couldn't read what I'd written. By the time I was four-and-a-half, I could count a bit, I could read a bit, I could write a bit. Amazing accomplishments which all my world applauded. I basked in the sun of approval. One evening when daddy carried me pick-a-back to bed he promised me a reward.

He listened to me saying my prayers.

Gentle Jesus, meek and mild
Look upon this little child.
Pity my simplicity,
Suffer me to come to thee

Daddy said "Amen" with me. Then he said "Lettice has a little brother, hasn't she?" She had and I didn't like him either.

"And Tony had a baby sister?"

She had. It was a cry-baby.

"Which would you like to have? A little brother or a little sister?"

"I'd like a big brother. He'd fight for me." Daddy laughed. "We can't have that. *You'll* be the big brother. What about you doing the fighting?"

I thought that over.

"I can fight. Miss Beal saw me and said I was a naughty, rough boy."

"She did, did she? Well, suppose we wait and see what Jesus sends us."

One rainy afternoon, Daddy took me to see what Jesus *had* sent us.

IT was a bundle in bed with Mummy. IT had a red face, wrinkled all over. IT was asleep.

Mother unwrapped one of ITs hands, which was just like the hand of one of Lettice's dolls. Mother said, "This is your new baby brother, Ronald. Daddy and I are going to call him Neville. Give me your finger . . . no, that one." She opened ITs hand and without opening ITs eyes, IT grasped my finger quite tightly.

"You looked just like him, darling, when you were born. There, now you've had a good look at him, I'll cover his head again."

Gran led me out.

Daddy came home with an armful of flowers and ran straight past me upstairs and closed the door.

My sky was clouded over. But like the dandelion, I knew where the sun was. It was in mother's bedroom and its name was Neville. I couldn't put that knowledge into words. I just knew, as the dandelion knows, where the sun was. I tried to win back the warmth which had been all mine. Gran was the only one who would listen to me reading my picture book. And she hadn't much time.

I had another idea.

I drew a house, the best I'd ever done. I made the windows as square as square could be and crayoned them in green. I drew the door in blue. I made the roof red and didn't forget to draw a curly wiggle of smoke coming out of the chimney pot. When I had finished my house, I drew a garden in front.

My childish heart contracted when I showed my picture to Mother. "It's very good darling." She said without looking at it. "The water's ready for baby's bath."

I did not know that what I was choking down wasn't tears but a monster with green eyes.

For as long as I could remember — a summer afternoon, a winter morning of the kind of time which is told by thistledown clocks and melting snowmen — I had been my own companion, needing no other in the world in which I lived and loved.

My grandmother Scriven, serenely settled in her little

red box-of-bricks, saw the hobgoblin the moment I took it to Ellers Road. She dealt with it in her own sweet way.

Where had I been all this time? Enlightenment warmed my grandmother's voice — of course, I couldn't tear myself away from my new brother. He was a nice little baby but he was too young to know how lucky he was to have a big brother like me to look up to. And it would be a long time, my grandmother warned me, before Neville was big enough to romp around and play with me.

Look at all the things I could do that Neville couldn't do.

My self-esteem ballooned.

The sun had come out again from behind the clouds.

My isolation as an only child was ended. I had two companions — Neville, called into being, like myself, by the love our parents bore one another; Neville, whose eyes, newly-focused, could not recognise me; and this green-eyed hobgoblin which I could not recognise.

Gran, my mother's mother, had given me all that she had given my mother — love unquestioning. This all-enfolding love she gave to me. Love unquestioning she gave to Neville in the moment when she first held him in her arms. It was a love so complete that it couldn't distinguish between the two of us. She did not notice the hobgoblin.

Neville was a baby.

It would be fun to play with him when he grew up. But when he did grow bigger it wasn't much fun. Mother was always on to me about being tidy. But when *Neville* threw all my toys out of the cupboard, she never said a word, even when he broke one of them. When *I* ticked him off, mother was cross with *me*.

Why did she always side with the little beast? Because

she loved him more than she loved me.

I didn't know what jealousy was. I only knew what I felt like. I didn't know the feeling's name was jealousy. It's difficult enough for a grownup to understand his emotions. A child can only feel them.

Mother never smacked Neville When, suddenly, she did I went hot all over. I rushed to stop her. "Don't smack him, don't smack him. He's my brother. Don't, Mummy, don't."

Was Neville glad he had a big brother to stick up for him? Not a bit of it. He knew why he'd been smacked.

So, in 1913, when he was two and I was six the bloodtie between us stood its first strain. And the world went very well then.

Chapter 3

THROUGH THE LETTER-BOX

About the time my grandmother had settled into her little red box-of-bricks I first became vaguely aware of the paper boy as a whistle coming up the scale of the garden path and going down it again. The whistle was punctuated in the middle by the CLACK of the letter-box flap.

One morning when I was playing in the hall the whistle stopped, a voice came through the letter-box. It said "I've bought yer *Rainbow*." The voice said a peculiar word which I couldn't make out.

My *Rainbow* was pushed onto the door-mat. The flap stayed open.

Through the slit I saw two bright eyes and part of a nose.

They vanished like a jack-in-the-box and the flap went snap.

I liked the *Rainbow* very much, especially Mrs. Bruin's school.

I liked Tiger Tim best. He wore a striped red and yellow suit and got into trouble because of all the tricks he played.

The next I saw of the paper boy was the day I heard him whistling and ran into the hall. The flap was open but all I could see was his ear. It turned at once into his eyes and a bit of his nose again. He said that peculiar sounding word again.

"Where've yer been? I thought yer was keen on this daft comic."

"I couldn't come, I was having my breakfast."

"'Avin' yer breakfas'? Mean ter say yer 'as yer breakfas' every day like all the other little twerps in the avenue?"

"What is a twerp?"

"You're one."

The word puzzled me, too. Could it be another name for 'boy'?

"Are you a twerp?" I asked.

"Am I 'eck. I can look after myself. Allus could. I don't get no breakfas'. Not unless I'm lucky. Me a twerp? 'Eck!"

The flap went snap.

Now I knew what the peculiar sounding word was. He was saying ''Eck.' I pulled the flap open from the inside. By standing on tiptoe I could see him as he went off whistling.

"'Eck." I yelled after him. I let the letter-box snap.

"'Eck," I said. It was a good word. It could mean anything you wanted it to mean. I said it to Gran when she asked me if I wanted her to read what the Bruin boys were doing this week.

I could read very well for four, I told Gran. I read to her to prove I could.

"Bim and Bam coughed a burglar stealing a ham 'eck."

"Caught, darling, not coughed," corrected Gran. "And you'd better not use vulgar words like heck in front of your mother."

I didn't know what vulgar meant but I didn't ask Gran, in case it meant what I thought it did.

I liked the paper boy.

'Eck, he allus looked after himself. Allus 'ad. He could go about barefoot, just as he pleased. So one day when I was in the back garden, I took off my shoes and socks to see what it was like. It felt lovely.

Mother caught me.

"Ronald. Put on your shoes at once."

"Mother, please. You let me play on the sands without them."

"That's different."

"'Eck, why is it different?"

"Ronald, have you been talking to that paper boy? I won't have you picking up vulgar expressions from street arabs. Never let me hear you using such words again."

What were street arabs? I knew by mother's tone that I'd best not ask her anything either. So next time the paper boy talked to me through the letter-box I asked him.

"Never 'eard on 'em."

"But I thought you knew *everything*?"

"I knows everythin' what goes on in mi own back yard an' a lot o' what goes on round 'ere. 'Eck, twerps like you knows nowt."

"I don't even know your name."

"I know yours. Ronald. Cissie name."

"Cissie is my auntie's name in South Milford."

The paper boy burst out laughing.

Now that I was a bit taller, I could look through the letter-box without standing on tiptoe. I could see his face. It was sharp and sort of pinched.

"It's a cissie name. Yer should 'a been giv'n a right name, like Fred."

I got it.

"*You're* Fred."

"That's me," said Fred.

I couldn't always go to the letter-box when Fred whistled through it. Gran didn't seem to mind my talking to him. Mother did. Mother could hear very well, like me. I was scared that one of these days she'd catch us, especially when I lost my temper with Fred when he teased me about my curls. I hated them. They were cissie. Fred said so. I hated them too because on Mother's 'At Home' days, which were on second Wednesdays, Mother would tug the comb through them extra hard.

"Stand still. Keep your feet together and mind your Ps and Qs when you offer the ladies sandwiches or cakes. And don't dare rumple your new suit before they arrive." 'At Homes' were beastly.

All the ladies were aunties. Real ones like my favourite Aunt Jess or pretend ones like Auntie Muriel who was mother's best friend. And all of them wanted to kiss me. When they did, their breath smelled of lady and powder and cream buns and scents which had somehow got mixed up with the cakes. Horrible. But they had to raise their veils before they could kiss me, which gave me the chance to be extra polite and dodge some of the kisses.

I could never dodge Auntie Muriel's and they smelled of the worse smell of all, scented cigarettes.

I found one of hers in an ashtray and tried to smoke it later, only it made me cough and was worse than the smoke smell in the drawing room. It made me feel bad. And they all talked all the time about votes for women, whatever they were.

Next time I talked to Fred I said "Mother's going to Auntie Muriel's this afternoon. And Gran always has a nap after lunch, will you come and play with me this afternoon?"

"You've gone crackers," Fred said. "I've got my evening paper round 'aven't I? They allus bring out specials on Saturday afternoons. Murders, bank robberies, suffragettes 'eaving bricks at bobbies. It's all mi eye and Betty Martin, but it catches the mugs every time."

"Can I come with you on the paper round? Nobody'll know. I could carry some of the papers."

"'Eck, it'd be the talk of the avenue, chump. We'd both be for it."

The nights grew a lot darker and Learie came down the avenue almost as soon as it was teatime. I loved to watch him opening the glass cages on top of all the lamp posts with his long magic wand and popping golden lights inside. They looked like yellow canaries which would sing away until Learie let them out again after breakfast time.

I knew it was going to be Guy Fawkes night soon because Daddy brought home a big box of fireworks he didn't think I knew about, but I saw him put it on top of the wardrobe. A few days later Fred whistled through the letter box.

"Remember me calling you a chump? It gives me an idea. You're allus asking to come out wi' me. Well, I'll whistle for yer at six o'clock sharp and you can slip out on the QT. It's mischief night."

Fred whistled and I went with him into a world I had never dreamed existed. A world of boys who all seemed to know Fred. Thin boys rubbed their white faces with soot. Under a lamp-post, Fred rubbed mine the minute we were clear of the house.

"Keep yer trap shut. They'll know yer a cissie if yer don't."

We whooped, we yelled, we screeched, we ran

through the town. They lifted gates from their posts. They rang people's doorbells and ran away. The first doorbell I rang I was nearly caught and would have been if Fred hadn't tripped the man who chased us. There was nothing vicious in our mischief on that night. Nobody put a cannon with a lighted fuse through anyone's letter-box.

None of us spoiled tomorrow's sport for others by setting light to a bonfire chumped for days beforehand.

After my narrow escape, wild with excitement I tried to do everything the others did. I helped to tie door handles to clothes posts and ran away whooping with the best of them.

Main streets, back streets, alleyways — we roamed them all. Had my feet been shod with Mercury's winged sandals that night, they could not have tired less. I had no more idea where I was than a drunk monk in a gutter. But I remember that I never left Fred's side and he looked after me like an elder brother.

How much older than I he actually was I don't know. His wizened face, black in Learie's lamplight, looked years older than mine. The hard, poverty-ground life he'd led had added those years to the head on his thin young shoulders.

Hardier, he was as excited as and no wearier than I. And unlike the symbolical drunk monk he had known exactly where he was.

He yelled suddenly "Scarper."

I remember how a man's hand had clamped my shoulder. A bull's eye beam had blinded me. Searching my identity.

"Now then, young 'un." A man's voice had said. "What's your name? Ah, yes, I know you. You're little Ronald Scriven, aren't you?"

Shock tied my tongue for a moment. Fred's voice jeered from the darkness between two lampposts.

"Ooo do yer think he is? Charlie Chaplin? 'Course he's Ronald Scriven. I was just taking him back to 'is 'ome."

The constable had enfolded himself in silence and the majesty of the law.

Father put me, bathed, pyjamaed and unscolded to bed. Had I been found two hours sooner, before anger could turn to relief, he'd have given me the dressing-down and mother the flat of her hairbrush treatment of my young lifetime.

I thought mother would demand and father agree that Fred should be punished.

"No, Gertie. At their age all boys are the same. From what I can make out, Fred looked after ours well enough. And he is a very good paper boy."

"We'd best keep mum an' lie doggo until it's blown over I reckon," was all Fred said next day.

For me, it blew over with the sky rockets, the floating, falling stars of the Roman candles and the spitfire sparks of the Catherine wheels.

It was mother's last 'At Home' until after Christmas, before Fred thought it safe to stop lying doggo.

"I just can't wait for Christmas, Fred. We're going to have a turkey and plum pudding and a Christmas tree and Santa Claus is going to climb down the chimney and fill my stocking."

"'Eck, there ain't no Santa Claus. Do yer still believe in that daft stuff? It's yer father dressed up in whiskers an' red flannel wot fills yer stocking."

I didn't believe a word of this shattering revelation. Hero though he was, I knew that Fred told great big fibs whenever he felt like it.

The morning before Christmas Eve, I told him something which had been going popple popple inside me like Harry Holgate's ginger beer ever since it had happened.

"Last night, Gran came home in a cab. The cabby carried a huge box of oranges for her. They were dropping about all over the path and Gran was singing."

"What was the old lass singing?"

"A lovely song. 'Tara-ra Boom-de-ay'."

"Pissed," said Fred, as one who has had his diagnosis confirmed by a second opinion.

"Fred. We've got tons of oranges. Gran's poorly this morning but I'm sure if I asked her she'll let you have as many as you like."

"Thanks fer nowt. If yer goes to t'city market on Christmas eve, late on, they'll gie yer owt that's left. Two years back they gied mi Dad a turkey. They locked him up on Boxing Day but not 'cause o' 't turkey. And I'll tell you summat else. That's why I go on 't paper round: I'm t' only breadwinner in t' family. Ma and me'll be rolling in it this Christmas. Nuns. They gie yer boots, suits, shirts, the lot. There's Mount St. Mary's and t' Sacred 'eart and Notre Dame. Best o' t' lot there's the Little Sisters of the Poor. They gie me boots for mi brothers and all."

"I didn't know you had any brothers."

"Chump, course I ain't. But I got a soap-box on wheels. The more boots and clobber I take to Uncle, the more brass he gies me. Twig?"

Fred had sharpened my wits. I knew that in Yorkshire brass meant money to everybody. I guessed that clobber meant clothes. But Fred had no more than brushed some of the dew off my innocence. And 'Uncle', in the sense Fred used the word, was one of the stumbling blocks of all translators. One of those words which read the same and sound the same in the two languages but do not mean the same thing.

"Your Uncle must be a meanie. I don't have to give mine anything if I want him to give me . . . ."

"'Eck, yer don't know yer born. Yer not just a twerp. Yer a proper Charlie.

"Uncle means a pawnbroker, chap who'll lend yer money on owt yer takes into 'is shop. If yer want it back again, it'll cost yer more brass nor he lent yer. If yer don't want it back he sells whatever it is. See? So 'e does alright for issen either way. My ma pops a gold locket she found in t' street on Monday and gets it back on Saturday out of my paper round. See?"

The hand-to-mouth economics of the very poor, whereby they become poorer and the rich richer, was beyond my comprehension then. Today — heck, it still baffles me.

The alien world Fred lured me into exploring had fascinated me because it *was* alien. Fred fascinated me because he understood that world's manners and customs so completely and could communicate them so vividly.

He had fascinated me above all because he *was* Fred.

In the nature of our relationship and my still dewy innocence, it never occurred to me that I likewise fascinated Fred. He couldn't communicate his intense curiosity about the world in which I lived.

To the avenue, he was just a barefoot street arab who happened to be their paper boy. To me, he was Fred. A sharp nose, a sharp eye and a sharp mind. Through these, he showed me his world in black-and-white. I could sense in a way, that in his world hunger gnawed at his belly. I couldn't understand why. My mind had not been sharpened by deprivation, but neither had my feelings been blunted into a taken-for-granted anonymity of the poor.

Fred was highly individual. Had any of the avenueites come across him in some neighbouring street without his satchel of newspapers, I don't think any one of them would have given him a second glance nor recognised him.

If his customers didn't know Fred, he knew them. Sniffs at a hundred kitchen doors, peeps through a hundred letter boxes had tantalised his imagination.

He had fascinated me as a guide into his penny plain, black-and-white world, taught me brilliantly the rudiments of its lingo. As a guide to my tuppence-coloured world I increasingly exasperated him. Once he'd grasped that all twerps like me had breakfast every day as a matter of course and three other meals on top of that, he stubbed his toe on another mystery.

With all that grub to 'ave a go at, why in 'eck didn't I stuff myself 'till I bust?

I told him the truth.

"Mother says I must leave the table while I'm still feeling just a bit hungry."

Completely baffled but half believing, Fred said "Must be barmy."

His mystification about my world was all the more puzzling because of a vogue among the young marrieds of 1913. Their parents had dined behind drapes so closely drawn that never a chink of light could be seen from the street. So fashionable avenueites at duskfall never drew their curtains at all.

Popping the late night finals through letter boxes, Fred loitered over his last paper round. What he saw amazed him. In lighted window after lighted window, there were whole families eating and drinking like billy-oh. There were servants bringing in dishes of soup big enough, he told me, to bath the baby in.

There were pictures on the walls, he said. Ladies clutching their bosoms as they read letters. Fred was fully prepared to watch a lady in shoulder-of-mutton sleeves leap to her feet, clutch her bosom and rip open an envelope.

They were barmy, the lot of them.

Some of them ate by candlelight, wot for? Fred knew for a fact they had electric lights. And what were the letters about anyway? Fred longed to know. He'd have found out too, if he'd had half a chance. Fred could read.

He was adept at spotting and dodging school attendance officers, after him on his afternoon rounds for turning an honest ha'p'ny instead of learning the three "r's".

Why *did* the avenue behave the way it did? What exasperated Fred the most was his knowledge that he'd never be able to find out from the inside.

The gentlemen who carved underdone sirloins of beef, the ladies who didn't clutch their bosoms hadn't a notion that their every movement was being closely observed by a sharp nose, a sharp eye and a sharp mind, sometimes from halfway up a tree in the autumn dusk of the avenue.

"We're going to the Pygmalion." said mother. "On the tram."

The tram was lovely.

PING PING, pinged the bell. When the tram swayed and lurched I felt my tummy sway too. I was so happy I closed my eyes but I soon opened them.

PING PING.

A few flakes of snow spattered the windows on the other side.

PING. I wanted to kneel on the seat and look out of the window behind me, but I knew what Mother would say to me if I did.

I rubbed my gloves together, which made me feel all creepy as one woollen glove rubbed the other. I snuggled against mother's warm furry coat. I pulled off one glove and slipped my hand inside her muff. It had a little pocket inside.

When we got off the tram, big snowflakes were falling. Look, there was Daddy to meet us. He picked up Neville.

The Grand Pygmalion of Monteith, Hamilton and Monteith burst upon me, the eighth wonder of my world. Looping wires rose, criss-cross to a glass cage high in the roof.

"I want a new veil," said Mother.

Daddy put a sovereign on the counter. The lady put it in a little wooden money box.

"Mummy, she's pulling the lavatory chain. Where is the lava . . . . ?"

"Don't be so rude," said mother. She smacked my hand. I didn't know why she was cross.

I watched the money-box whizz up to the glass cage. When it whizzed back again, I saw that somebody had put a lot more money in it, wrapped in a piece of paper.

"Now, Gertie, you take Neville in tow and meet me in half-an-hour in the grotto. Come on Ronald."

All the way down the stairs there were toys lining every step. Forts. Drums. Indian wigwams. Dolls. And at the bottom of the stairs the Eiffel tower made with Meccano, with a lift going up and down — inside it, flashing lights. There was an elephant on wheels.

Daddy pulled me away. "Come along."

There were simply regiments of toy soldiers in every

kind of uniform you ever saw. I didn't know which to look at next.

Daddy did.

"Gun mules. Now this is clever."

There were six mules and three of them had wheels you could take off and the other three had gun barrels which fitted on to the wheels. You fired the steel shells by pulling back a spring and letting it go.

"You can go where you please, you can climb up the trees," said Daddy, "but you can't get away from the guns."

"I want them. I want them."

"We'll see what Santa Claus has to say about that," said Daddy.

Then I saw it and forgot about everything else. A motor car. A beautiful, beautiful, beautiful big blue motor car. It was big enough for me to get into the front seat and it had a back seat too. It had red mudguards and brass headlamps with real glass in them. There were pedals to drive it, a steering-wheel and a horn. I climbed into the seat. PAAAP. PAAAP. PAAAP.

Daddy tweaked my ear.

"Out you come. I expect Mother will be waiting for us."

I looked over my shoulder until I couldn't see the beautiful motor car any more.

Mummy and Neville were waiting for us in the grotto. And there was Santa Claus himself. He was in a red robe with snow round the edges and he had a long white beard.

I was so excited that I hardly had enough breath to whisper in his ear. "Please, I want that beautiful motor car."

All I could think about until Christmas eve was its steering wheel and its headlamps, its red mudguards and the lovely lovely sound of its horn.

The minute I woke up, I scrambled to the foot of our bed. Santa Claus had been. I dragged both the stockings over the quilt and tried to guess what was in mine by feeling the lumps inside it. Something very hard. A paint box. Neville had curled up in my place and he was still warm and sleepy when I pushed him back where he belonged and dumped his stocking on top of him. He sat up suddenly when he realised what it was.

We pulled everything out and I could tell by touch the apple and the orange and the new penny. Right in the toe of each stocking was a sugar mouse. Neville started nibbling his and he'd nibbled all of it except the candlewick tail when Daddy switched on the light.

He kissed us both. "Happy Christmas, Ronald. Happy Christmas, Neville." We hugged him hard as we could.

"Happy Christmas, Daddy," we both shouted.

He jigged Neville up and down on his back.

"I want a piggy-back too."

Daddy pranced downstairs, both of us clinging on to his shoulder, and into the dining room.

There it was on the rug in front of the fire. My motor car.

The pedals bit my bare feet. PAAP. PAAP. PAAP. PAAP. I turned the steering wheel.

"Let me get in. Let me get in." Neville tried to climb into the back seat by way of the bumper.

"Get off my motor car. It's mine. It's mine. Daddy, make him leave my motor car alone."

Neville howled. Mother hurried in. She picked up Neville. "Darling, let Ronald have it all to himself for a while," she said.

Neville kicked himself out of her arms and drummed on the carpet with his heels and howled and howled.

On New Year's Day, Janus looked backwards, shrugged and looked forwards. He saw ahead, on the 4th August 1914, a contemptible little army mustering to fight a war which would be over by Christmas.

Did he glance backwards at Alfred Lord Tennyson scribbling:

Let us swear an oath and keep it with an equal mind
In the hollow Lotus Land to live and lie reclined
On the hills like gods together, careless of mankind?
I do not know.

Spring returned, bringing with her seven candles for my birthday cake.

In a quiet corner of a green and pleasant, if not a lotus, land I drove my motor car up and down Harehills Avenue.

I didn't mind Neville's riding in the back seat, now. But I did get fed up with the extra weight I had to pedal.

June came, bringing to England a mild heat-wave and to a small white town in the Balkans, the heir to the Austro-Hungarian throne.

The town was Sarajevo, a place few in England had ever heard of, outside the Foreign Office.

There the Archduke Franz Ferdinand was assassinated by a student, Gabriel Princip, in an attempt to secure Serbia's independence from the ramshackle empire romanticised by Anthony Hope as Ruritania.

The assassin's finger squeezing the trigger had fired the first shot of the 1914 war.

Fred sold a few score extra copies of the special which for once had genuinely sensational news.

The dove of peace continued to coo in England.

Chapter 4

BLOOD BROTHERS

The cab wheels went bump over the cobblestones.

I sang inside my head. Go on, go on, go on. We'll be late. We'll miss the train. We'd left Neville with Gran. Only me with Daddy and Mummy. I was hot with excitement.

"Marsh Lane," said the cab driver. Daddy helped Mummy out.

My cheeks felt suddenly cool as I climbed three flights of dark stairs.

"Daddy, we've missed it. The train's gone."

"Not it," said Daddy. "I've looked it up in Bradshaw. Our train for South Milford will depart at 11.24 on the dot."

He took my hand as we went into the booking hall.

"Come along with me to the ticket office."

He pushed a sovereign through the hole in the window. The ticket clerk, with a pale, calm, bearded face, was in no hurry.

"The train's coming. I can hear it. Oh, hurry, hurry, Daddy."

Daddy only laughed and strolled out on to the platform. Sure enough a train was in, but it was panting away beside the opposite platform. Daddy dumped his Gladstone bag beside a tall very red chocolate machine. He sat down beside mother on a green seat.

"Daddy. May I have a penny to put in the slot?"

The brass handle of the little drawer was quite hot. Nestle's Swiss Milk Chocolate made my tongue melt. The train moved away from the other platform. When would ours come in?

I read the advertisements on the other platform. OWBRIDGE'S LUNG TONIC. STEPHEN'S BLUE-BLACK INK. THEY COME AS A BOON AND A BLESSING TO MEN, THE PICKWICK, THE OWL AND THE WAVERLY PEN.

A signal arm dropped.

Our train was coming.

We had a compartment all to ourselves. I knelt on my corner seat and pressed my nose to the window. "We're going, we're going, we're going."

The platform and the booking office slid backwards. Red sparks floated past my window. The train rushed into darkness.

"Marsh Lane tunnel," said Daddy. "It's the first ever built for rail traffic only."

Our train burst out of the black tunnel straight into the sun.

It rushed past houses and walls and back gardens — faster, faster, faster. It was rushing past green fields. There were toy Noah's ark animals pretending to eat the grass. They came to life. Some of them kicked up their heels and galloped away from our train.

Toy stations became real ones. CROSSGATES. GARFORTH. MICKLEFIELD. SOUTH MILFORD.

45

"Here we are. We're here, Daddy."

A man was waiting for us. "Morning Mr. Jack," he said. "Morning Ma'am."

"Good morning, Tom. This is Ronald."

"Aye?" said Tom, "Doctor's on his rounds in the new motor car he's bought. So I've brought the gig."

I could see over the hedges.

The sun was as hot as hot. But it had been snowing. All the leaves on the hedges were white, I pointed out.

"Not snow, Ronald. Dust. By Jove, Tom, it's good to be in the country."

We passed a house. On the lawn was a tent made of sticks and leaves. Two little girls popped out of it and waved. So I waved back.

"Steady, Judy girl," said Tom.

"The Terrace," said Daddy. "We're here." Wide green gates were propped open at each end of a long row of tall, grey stone houses. A gravel drive separated the house from a lawn as long as the terrace. It had no dividing hedges.

"Whoa, Judy."

We'd got to South Milford but there was nothing to do. I liked lunch and Auntie Ciss asked me if I would have a second helping of strawberries and cream. I wanted to, terribly, but I said no thank you because of what mother had taught me about good manners.

"He hasn't much of an appetite," said Auntie Ciss. "The heat, I suppose."

"Don't fidget," said mother.

"No, mother. Please may I leave the table?"

"You may not."

They were all talking all the time. Auntie Ciss had a dog called Chang. It sat up and begged.

There were two pictures on the wall. Some calves

coming down a land and the same calves in a field.

There was nothing to *do* in South Milford. I couldn't even look out of the window without wriggling round in my chair.

"It's clear Harold won't be back for lunch," said Auntie Ciss. "Ronald may as well go out and play with Wilfred, the boy next door."

Halfway up the only tree on the lawn was a boy in a tattered and torn brown suit. He had a catapult and let go with it. His second shot got me on the cheek and stung. The boy shinned down and went for me. We rolled over and over on the grass kicking and pummeling each other.

Now a real dog joined in, yelping. Chang. Our dogfight had become a three-cornered one. A woman's voice shouted: "Hi. Wilfred. Just wait till I get my hands on you."

Wilfred said "C'mon. Cut and run. Follow me."

I heard mother and Auntie Ciss call. I cut and ran after Wilfred.

Wilfred was over the iron railings quick as a monkey. He'd ripped his velvet suit some more. He looked back and called, "C'mon." I followed him unquestioningly.

Wilfred Kemp, even as a boy, had the panache of a born leader. His voice had a slight Irish underlilt, an urgency which compelled one to want to do whatever Wilfred wanted to do. He could charm a charm of goldfinches off a bough.

It was a long time afterwards that Wilfred told me why he had set about me. His mother had dressed him in a new Little Lord Fauntleroy-style suit which revolted all the nobler aspirations of Wilfred's soul. He had shinned into the tree in order to inflict mayhem on the brown velvet and maltreat the lace collar

47

and cuffs. So he would never have to wear the hateful suit again. A strategist, he had armed himself with a catapult and hard twisted paper pellets to keep his elder sisters, Phyllis and Muriel, at bay. When I came out of Number 1, the shame of being seen in such an outfit by a fellow boy had red-ragged Wilfred to instant attack.

The old surgery was set back a few yards from the main road. The wall took a sweep to the left. Behind the house were the stables. From the end of the wall it was only a step up to the roof of an old railway carriage lifted off its bogies and set there to store wheelbarrows, scythes, sacks of hops and old carriage lamps. It was Tom Baker's handyman's arsenal. An apple tree overshadowed the coach. Wilfred and I munched apples larger, greener and more sour than crabs. They were delicious.

From the command post the strategist considered his campaign. Next to the loose boxes was a wooden harness room. Beyond that, a small orchard. A brindled bulldog, with one ear tattered, snored in the shade of the harness room. I eyed it fearfully. Not Wilfred.

"Good old Buller." Wilfred tickled the massive underjaw. "Your auntie won't have him about the house. She says he smells. The village kids used to throw stones at him. Poor Buller won't hurt a fly . . . "

"Come on."

I ran after him through the orchard. A green gate separated it from the paddock.

"I'm Robinson Crusoe," said Wilfred. "This is the stockade I've built to keep the savages out. You're Man Friday. The savages are after you. I shoot them. BANG. BANG. BANG. BANG. I've killed them. You tremble. Go on, tremble. You put my foot on your head."

Wilfred's imagination carried me along in its train. We'd gone through the paddock.

Beyond it was a railway embankment pierced by a narrow tunnel. Water dripped dankly from the roof. Through the blur of light at the other end we came out on to the bank of a cressy stream.

"The Amazon," shouted Wilfred. "No white man has ever explored its headwaters. We will."

I followed him doggedly. We took off our shoes, tied the laces and swung them round our necks. We went joyously, splashing our way up the Amazon.

Meeting Wilfred was shaking off all the restraints of my upbringing.

Fred the paper boy had loosened some of them. Wilfred gloriously burst them asunder.

Up stream, past the osier beds, we stood still. Minnows nibbled our ankles.

Wilfred hissed in my ear, "Alligators. The only way to kill them is to shoot them through their eyes. BANG. BANG. BANG. There. I've saved your life."

And suddenly we were no longer in the upper reaches of the Amazon but on the Spanish main.

"I'm Drake," said Wilfred, "I'm going to singe the beard of the King of Spain. You're the King of Spain."

The compelling, commanding Irish lilt of Wilfred's voice spellbound me. And binding, set me free from resentment. Resentment against being always told not to do that. Told to keep my feet together, to say please and thank you. To keep quiet, to sit still when I wanted to wriggle, and always to behave myself.

The odd thing was that I didn't resent being ordered about by Wilfred. Like all great leaders, he was generous. "You've saved my life," he said when I shot Sitting Bull as he was about to bury his tomahawk in

Wilfred's scalp. "Now we must be blood brothers."

He opened his pocket knife.

"It's very sharp," he said. "If I press it on your thumb, quite hard, it won't cut as long as I keep the blade steady. When I move it, the blade will cut."

It did and the sight of the blood upset me more than the sting of the cut.

"Now you cut my thumb," said Wilfred. He stuck out his thumb. "Go on. Cut."

We mixed our life blood together and Wilfred found a dock leaf to wrap round the cuts. We bound the dock leaves with strips we tore from the hanky I happened to have in my pocket.

"Now we're blood brothers," said Wilfred, "we must go through hell and high water for each other. Now and forever."

In that golden afternoon of the kingdom of boyhood, time was not, and place was what Wilfred said it was.

Bee orchised, milkmaided, campioned — the English fields were as boundless as the prairies where the flower-fed buffaloes roamed.

If Wilfred said a rolling meadow was the Spanish Main, why cows in the next pasture were treasure galleons for Drake in the *Golden Hind* to plunder, and I, following in his wake, to harass.

The greensleeve hedges blended their honeysuckled breath with the smell of new-mown hay.

I did not know the names of more than a dozen flowers, half a dozen birds. Wilfred, country-bred, knew them all.

He sank a galleon with a parting broadside and pounced on a small, bright red flower.

"Scarlet Pimpernel."

Madame Guillotine was knitting as the tumbrils rolled across the Paris cobblestones.

Alternately, she counted her stitches and the heads which were lopped. Little did the *sans culottes* know that in fact the ghoul of the guillotine was the elegant, indolent Sir Percy Blakeney.

Little did they realise that I, his faithful companion, was waiting, just around the corner, with a post-chaise to whisk the next rescued French aristocrat to a Channel port and safety.

Waiting for Sir Percy, my heart throbbing with admiration of his daring. I noticed that my bandaged thumb was throbbing too.

"So is mine," said Wilfred, returning abruptly from Calais. "It's the heat probably. I know. Tom's got some horse liniment in the harness room."

Even in a timeless afternoon, shadows lengthen. The stableyard was deep in them. The harness room was locked.

"Mother," said Wilfred gloomily "will be furious. Come on. We'll go home by the back lane."

In the deepening dusk, as we approached the back of The Terrace, an owl hooted and its hunting call was answered by its mate.

Wilfred was inspired. He hooted back.

"That's to be our secret Indian call," he said. "Hoot." I hooted.

"When I'm in bed tonight, I'll stick my head out of the window and make our call. Mind you answer it."

Hooting at one another from behind the trees we ran the rest of the way home.

There were lights in groundfloor windows. As I opened the back door Ivy, Auntie Ciss's cook, pounced on me.

"My word, you're for it, you young limb. Your father . . . what have you done to your thumb?"

Uncle Harold took me to his surgery.

"Well admiral, let's have a look at it." He didn't make me feel frightened, but the surgery did. It had a glass case with rows of awful looking shiny instruments in it. My thumb suddenly stopped hurting. Uncle Harold began to unwrap the grubby bandage.

"H'm. I shan't hurt you but this stuff's going to sting a bit. What did you do it with? Barbed wire? A bit of broken glass? Doesn't look like either."

While he swabbed the wound, I told him about Wilfred and the cuts and mixing our blood and becoming blood brothers.

"Indian braves, eh? Now's the time to prove you're brave." Ointment, lint and bandage made me feel a wounded hero.

My bedroom had a dormer window. In the half-moonlight, night scents flowed through the room. Far away I heard a locomotive whistle, then the clack, clack, clack as the waggons caught up with each other. Closer at hand a tawny owl hooted as though answering the locomotive. I sat up. Wilfred's secret call?

The genuine signal silenced the locomotive and the hunting owl and my fears that Wilfred had forgotten our pact. I stuck my head out of the casement and hooted back.

"Your uncle came and made me have my thumb done," called Wilfred. "I'll make our secret call first thing tomorrow. Like this, Woo, woo, W' WOOOOOO."

Presently, with the half-moon, Night lit the pipe of peace.

Chapter 5

THE DEATH OF NELSON

Sunday breakfast was going to go on and on for ever.
And Wilfred had given our secret call twice already.

Warm air wafted in from the open window behind me.

A cold wave of despair flowed over me. A blackbird
raised his alarm call.

"Please may I . . . . "

"No," said mother, "You may not."

Wilfred would grow tired of waiting for me. I wanted
to rush outside before he was over the hills and far
away.

"Have some toast and marmalade," said Auntie Ciss.
"No? You might as well. We're not setting out for church
for at least twenty minutes."

Church? *CHURCH?* The dark night of the soul
overcame the June morning.

I knelt on a hassock. No use praying to God to cut
the service short. He wouldn't. He'd listened to psalms,
sermons and Hymns A and M for millions of years and
still he wanted more. Didn't God ever get sick of so
many mouldy old hymns?

I sat down. Mother nudged me and I stood up. "Praise him, praise him, praise him, praise him." Wilfred didn't have to praise him.

Mother nudged me again. "Sit down," she said.

Uncle Harold read the second lesson. Because it was Uncle Harold I listened, but I couldn't make head or tail of it except that God wasn't very pleased with somebody.

"Have your penny ready," said Mother. "They're coming round with the collection plate."

At last the organ began to make organ noises and it was all over.

Would you believe it, Mr. Barry, the Rector, nipped round to the porch and was wasting more time shaking hands with everybody.

Outside at last. My heart gave a great big bump, from a clump of yew trees by the gates, I heard Wilfred hoot. So did everybody else.

That was all right. Only my blood brother and I knew what it meant. Mother gave me a sharp look. I tried to look as though I hadn't heard anything. If they didn't think I wanted to rush off, perhaps they wouldn't stop me.

Then another blow fell.

"You and Gertie make your own arrangements for after lunch," said Auntie Ciss. "I've planned a treat for Ronald. I'm taking him along to Willow Cottage to play with those nice little Middlebrook girls." Girls? Gosh! How absolutely awful.

"This is Claire," said Mrs. Middlebrook. "This is Peggy. Now you two. Ronald doesn't know anything about the country. He's a town boy. Take him along and show him what the country's like."

Peggy was the bold one. She grabbed my hand. Shy Claire took the other. They led me along the banks of a stream.

There were thousands of daisies in the field by the stream.

"I know," said Peggy. "We'll teach Ronald how to make daisy-chains."

Daisy-chains. Mother had taught me how to make daisy-chains long ago. Claire hung the first one round my neck. Wilfred, wherever he was and whatever he was doing, wasn't making daisy-chains.

"Look, Ronald, those are swallows," said Peggy. "They're hatching out their second brood."

Claire spotted an old pan close to the bank, Peggy lay down and, dipping her hand in the water, lifted it out. Out of it wriggled a snake.

"Don't touch it," I yelled. "It's a snake. It may be poisonous."

The girls giggled. "You are funny, Ronald," said Claire. "It's only an eel."

"Catch it," shouted Peggy.

It wriggled through my fingers like a huge, cold, slimy worm. I snatched off my cap and grabbed it through the cloth.

"Come on. Come on."

We ran into the yard at the back of the cottage. There was a big green water-butt at the foot of some stone steps where I plopped it into the water.

"Hurray. Hurray," shouted Peggy. "Now we'll fish for it."

With a willow rod, a length of string and a bent pin we fished in turn for that eel all the afternoon. Peggy kept dashing off to find worms to bait the hook. None of us caught that eel.

We had a lovely tea under the weeping willow on the lawn. When Auntie Ciss called for me, Claire, shy Claire, flung her arms about my neck and said, "Ronald is my sweetheart."

I lay awake that night quaking. What if Wilfred got to hear about Claire?

Daddy said next morning, "Mother and I are going back to Leeds. You are going to stay in South Milford for a fortnight's holiday. We can't leave Neville too long with Gran you know. Now be a good boy and have a happy time."

It's too good to be true, I told myself. It's too good to be true. A whole fortnight with Wilfred.

In the morning rain poured down the windowpanes. No use asking Aunt Ciss if I could go out. I picked up my *Swiss Family Robinson*. I liked the book but there was such a lot of reading in it.

I saw Wilfred dash past the window. He was ringing the doorbell. He was saying to Aunt Ciss, "Please, Mrs. Radcliffe, Mother says it's too wet to play out and can Ronald come to our house?"

Wilfred's house felt very different from Uncle's. I noticed it the instant I'd wiped my feet on the mat. "Come on, I've something to show you."

On every wall of Wilfred's breakfast room were what looked like big, closed books. Wilfred pulled out the first book "Shut your eyes," he said.

I screwed my eyes tight.

"Now open them." I saw the pages weren't pages but glass. Behind the glass were rows of butterflies. Butterflies such as I could never have imagined.

Every butterfly looked alive and was at least six inches across. Their wings were of marvellous colours. Scarlet that almost hurt my eyes. Blue which made them ache.

Wilfred opened case after case.

"Whose are they, Wilfred?" I asked.

"They're my father's. He sent them from 'Frisco, where the earthquake was. Where the gold mines are."

Gold mines. I was too dumbfounded to say anything.

"When he strikes it lucky," said Wilfred "he's going to come home with a fortune. There are golden gates in 'Frisco. Simply everything's made of gold."

I believed him, though I'd no notion of where 'Frisco was.

"My father," said Wilfred "rides on a coach and horses straight through a hole cut in a tree."

I felt a sudden, awful, treacherous spasm of disbelief. Fred told great big fibs whenever he felt like it. I'd believed everything my new hero had told me. He wasn't at all like Fred.

"Come on," said Wilfred, guessing what I was thinking. "I'll show you."

He led me into the next room. There was a table set for lunch. On the wall was a photograph of a coach and horses being driven through a tunnel cut in a tree.

"What did I tell you?"

There were six ladies inside the coach. On top of it were four men. Wilfred pointed to the one sitting next to the driver.

"That's my father. He's on his way to the gold mines."

After that, I never disbelieved a word Wilfred said to me.

Wilfred's was a wonderful house.

"Children," called Mrs. Kemp. "Lunch time."

Wilfred's sisters Phyllis and Muriel came in carrying food from the kitchen.

"Does anyone know where Clifford is?" asked Mrs.

Kemp.

"Cliff's in the attic," said Wilfred, "galvanising a frog."

"Run upstairs and tell him to stop it," said Mrs. Kemp, "it's lunch time."

Clifford was nearly a man. He had a deep voice. After lunch he asked me if I would like to watch the frog being galvanised. I could hardly wait. In the attic, I was surprised to find that the frog was dead.

"This is a Leclanche battery," said Clifford. "I've connected these wires to the frog's legs. Watch me. Now I'll switch on the battery."

The dead frog began to twitch and jerk. Watching it kick its green legs made me laugh though I didn't really want to.

After tea the air felt very stuffy and sticky. Phyllis, Wilfred's oldest sister, went over to the gramophone.

"Open the window wider," said Mrs. Kemp. "I think there's going to be a thunderstorm." Phyllis put on the Merry Widow Waltz. The music sounded as though it came from over the water. A long way away thunder began to rumble. Then sheet lightning shimmered all over the sky. The music and the lightning danced with each other in the summer rain. It was only a passing shower.

The grass in the paddock behind the old surgery had grown more lush. Judy cropped it, and Snowball, Aunt Ciss's old hunter, now pensioned off. Out of the rough pasture Tom had made a tennis court. Netting draped over hedge stakes protected the court. At one end of it was a summerhouse. Its door had once been the drawing room of the old surgery in the days of Llewellyn Radcliffe. Ciss had disliked that door so Tom had fitted it to the summerhouse.

He was marking out the lines of the tennis court when Wilfred and I raced each other across the paddock.

"Hardy," Wilfred's voice commanded. I shot into the summerhouse after him.

"Arethusa," said Wilfred, "has sighted the combined French and Spanish fleets off Trafalgar. I'm Lord Nelson. Clear the decks of *Victory* for action."

"Aye, aye, sir." I obeyed.

Nelson had already opened a long wooden locker which held croquet mallets, iron hoops, old tennis rackets and coloured croquet balls.

"Cannon balls," said Nelson, "fire them by the gun ports. Rake them with broadsides. DEATH TO THE FRENCH."

We dropped croquet balls BONG on to the wooden floor. They made a splendid booming noise.

"Boarding parties stand by. Grip your cutlasses in your teeth. Kill as many of the Frenchies as you can in the shortest possible time."

BOOM. BOOM. BOOM.

In the thick of the action, Nelson staggered.

"I am mortally wounded, Hardy. A French rifleman has put a bullet through the star of my Order of the Garter. I am dying." He slumped to the quarter deck. "Kiss me, Hardy."

Sorrowfully I leaned over Nelson and kissed him.

"England expects," said the dying Admiral, "that every man this day will do his duty. I have done mine. The French are licked to a frazzle. Pickle my body in a cask of brandy and take it back to England."

He raised himself on one elbow.

"Tow me up the Thames in a black barge with black cars. All London will line the river to see me taken to

St. Pauls. See to it that they do, Hardy. Farewell."

Stock still, I waited for the death of Nelson. Wilfred sprang to his feet. "Stand to attention."

Straight backed side by side we stood. We sang Rule Britannia,
Britannia rules the waves.
Britons never, never, never shall be slaves.

Of a sudden, it felt hot, dry and close in the summer-house. Wilfred felt it too, he leaned against the door. Its central panel was a muddy brown colour. It was bordered by squares of glass. They were red, blue and yellow. Wilfred turned and looked through a red square.

"Snowball," he said, "has turned pink. The sky's purplish."

I joined Wilfred. I looked through the blue pane. "He isn't now," I said. "I've turned Snowball pale blue." I looked up at the sky, it was dark blue, nearly like night. I looked at the grass, it was brownish.

I looked through the yellow pane. Snowball turned pale gold. The sky had changed to orange. When I looked at the sun, oh, all the world was suddenly double sunshine.

If there were shadows, they had within them the bloom of light. The battles we fought together were battles long ago. As it was for me, so it was for my country in the days when August Bank Holiday 1914 was a date to look forward to.

Looking backwards, my memory has cast its light in double sunshine on those boyhood days with Wilfred.

Chapter 6

THE WIND AND THE RAIN

I was making a ship with my Meccano, very quietly.

I had to be very, very quiet because Mummy was ill and Gran was upstairs looking after her.

I heard the letter-box go SNAP twice. Fred's signal. I rushed very quietly to the door.

"'Ere," said Fred. "I've brought yer *Comic Cuts*, see."

"Talk quietly, Mummy's poorly."

"I know what's up with 'er. 'Ad all 'er teeth out. I saw 'er. Bleeding like a stuck pig."

"She's not. She's not."

Fred whispered. "Gie's a fag."

"A fag?"

"A gasper. A cigarette, chump."

"I can't. I haven't got any."

"Pinch one of yer ma's."

"She doesn't smoke."

"She does. I seen 'er, fibber."

I didn't say anything. I felt bad.

"Go on. Or I won't gie yer any more *Comic Cuts*."

I felt bad about that too.

Daddy liked me to read the *Rainbow*. It wasn't as funny, though, as *Comic Cuts*. Weary Willie and Tired Tim were funny.

I knew Mummy smoked but never when Daddy was at home. I said, "I can't get you one now Fred. I know where she keeps the box. I'll get you one when Gran lets me go upstairs to see her."

"Mind yer think on then. Or yer get no more comics on the QT. 'Eck, it's started to rain. I'm off."

Doctor Roper came and went upstairs to see Mummy.

In the afternoon Aunt Jess came and when she went back to Ellers Road she took Neville with her. "I want to see Grandma too," I said.

"No, dear," said Gran. "When you're both together you're too noisy. Neville's only a toddler and doesn't understand that Mummy can't do with you both rushing around, making a noise. You're a big boy of eight and know better."

I waved goodbye as they went off in the rain.

"Come in and shut the door," said Gran. I did. Then I looked through the letter box, but there was nobody going by.

I began to feel hungry. Gran made tea.

"Is Mummy better?"

"No dear. Not yet," she said.

I went back to the letterbox. The wind came through and smelled of rain. It made me want to go out in my wet-weather things and play. I asked Gran if I could?

"No, you're not going out. I've no time to watch what you're up to, and have you running in and out with wet boots."

"Can I go up and see Mummy then? Just for five minutes."

"No dear. Now why don't you read your favourite

Robinson Crusoe?"

I suddenly remembered *Comic Cuts*. I took it out of its hiding place and hid it again between the pages of *Robinson Crusoe*.

When Gran took me to bed I asked her when Daddy would be home. "Long after you're asleep. He has to work very late because of the war."

I missed Fred next morning because Gran was late with breakfast. "Is Mummy better?"

"Not yet dear. Now what is that you're making with your Meccano?"

"A ship," I said. "But there aren't enough nuts for the bolts." Gran went into the kitchen. Daddy had told me, "When you fasten two strips together, always let them overlap each other by three holes. That way, two nuts and bolts lock the strips fast. The whatever you are making will have both strength and safety. Things a good engineer never forgets."

I didn't forget. Now I found out for myself that if I used only one nut and bolt and screwed them very tightly, I could finish my ship. It looked grand when I finished it. When Daddy came home, I thought, I'll show him how clever I've been. Remembering to be tidy, I put it all away in my cupboard. Then I had nothing to do.

I went to the letter-box. It was raining hard again. A group of the Royal Horse Artillery trotted past. The gun limbers went waggle-waggle. The guns. The guns. The horses were very wet and steaming. The riders sat up as straight as the rain was falling. They were whistling as they rode. It's a long way to Tipperary. The guns. I couldn't get them out of my mind. I kept on rushing back to the letterbox hoping they'd be coming back again but they didn't. But I knew where they'd gone. To France. To fight Kaiser Bill.

The wind had got up some more. It blew the rain into the letter-box. Then I saw a man hurrying past with his coat collar up. I knew at once he was a German spy trying to hide his face. He was hurrying to tell the Huns where the barracks were. But I got there before them. Wilfred was in command of the guns.

"I am Sir Douglas Haig. The Huns are going to attack. My orders are 'Defend England to her last man and the last gun. Shoot them to blazes.'"

Captain Wilfred Kemp saluted.

I led him and his gunners at full gallop down the avenue. Horse, foot and artillery, the enemy poured down on us from the parade. "You're wounded, Sir Douglas," cried Captain Kemp. I shouted, "What does a bullet in the leg matter. Blaze away, the guns." At the signal of my outflung sword the battery wheeled into line unlumbered and let go. My horse shot, I led on foot the bayonet charge which wiped them out to the last Boche. But where was Captain Kemp? "His last words," said the soldier who had seen him fall, "were 'Tell my commanding officer I died for England'."

I was so moved that I hardly noticed the bruise on my right hand caused by hitting the hall table when I swung the guns into line.

Presently I went back to the letter-box to watch the rain washing away the blood from the battlefield.

I wondered if Neville had seen them. He loved horses. I called out "Gran. When is Neville coming home?"

Gran said, "Don't shout."

"Will Mummy let *him* see her when he does?" I felt positive sure that Mummy would. "She will. I know she will."

"Silly boy. Mummy will see both of you as soon as she's better. Oh dear, I wish it would stop raining. I'll

take you to the shops with me tomorrow if it's fine."
Gran went upstairs.

I looked out of the letter-box. A milkman came along
All the cans in his cart rattled. I watched him carrying
his can to a house across the avenue. The wind suddenly
went WOOOF. It blew a piece of paper on to the horse's
nose. Off it trotted without him.

A rag-and-bone man went by, pushing a handcart. He
shouted "Anny-ol'-iron, anny-ol'-iron? Rags-bones-er-
borrels?"

A car came up the avenue quite fast. It sloooshed a
big pool of water all over him. The rag and bone man
shook his fist. I laughed, he looked so funny.

Then I saw a man with a big black umbrella. He
started to cross the road. The wind blew a big howl and
the umbrella flew inside out. Then the wind sent his hat
spinning over the hedge into someone's garden. The man
looked so silly when he tried to chase it and tripped
over his broken umbrella.

Such a lot of things were happening that I stayed at
the letter-box all day, except when I went to eat. I was
watching a lady pulling a pram backwards against the
wind when I suddenly sneezed and the letter-box flap
snapped down.

My eyes felt runny, I fished in my pocket for my hanky.
I thought gosh I'm going to have another nasty cold. I
went and sat by the fire. I remembered *Comic Cuts* and
picked up *Robinson Crusoe*. Weary Willie was very fat.
Tired Tim was thin. I rubbed my eyes with my fists. I
coudn't make out which was which. The room felt suddenly hot. I wanted Daddy to come home. I wanted to show
him my ship. I looked again at Weary Willie and Tired
Tim. They seemed to have sort of blurred together.

Gran called "Bedtime, Ronald. It's getting late."

I couldn't remember ever before wanting to go to bed.

In the morning I had a tight feeling in my head. My tummy felt icy cold inside. I shivered. My eyelids were all stuck up. I didn't want to get out of bed. I thought I heard Gran calling me but I wasn't sure.

Somehow I got into my clothes. All except my socks. I bent down to pick them up. As I stood up a frightful pain stabbed me right inside my left ear.

I ran to the stairs. Gran was half way up them. She was cross.

"I've been calling you these last ten minutes. Don't you know what a lot I have to do? Your breakfast . . . "

She put her hand under my chin and lifted my face.

"Ronald. Oh, Ronald. Your eyes. Your poor eyes. Whatever's happened to them?"

She put her arms round me and took me downstairs. She led me to the sofa and put cushions under my head. I turned my head and the pain stabbed again.

I cried out. "My ear. My ear. The pain's in my ear, it's burning, burning."

"My poor lamb, my poor lamb. Your eyes are as red as raw beef. Oh, what *can* I do?"

She must have been utterly confused between what her own eyes told her and what I was sobbing.

She said "I must do something." She wasn't there any more. Then she was. She laid a warm, wet cloth over my eyes.

"There, there. That will soothe your eyes."

I snatched it off. "Take it away. My eyes don't hurt. It's my ear, my ear hurts right through inside my head."

She went away. She came back. "I know what to do for earache, hot onion wrapped in the heel of a stocking. There."

The onion felt red-hot. I felt it burning against my

left ear. The stabbing pain stabbed again, and again, and again. The pain felt red, red as a coal in the fire. And the fire burned deep inside my ear.

I heard somebody scream. The last thing I remember afterwards was knowing that I was hearing myself screaming inside my own head.

Lucid intervals of delirium, recollected later mixed by memory with disconnected fragments of delirium itself.

I lost time, I lost place, I lost people. All was confusion. I drifted towards the edge of darkness. But the darkness was not utter and from it a current of consciousness drifted me to the edge of light. I was in my own bed again. When someone took my hands in his I knew they were Daddy's hands.

How long it took that current of consciousness to carry me past the edge of light and into light itself I do not know. My most desolate and abiding memory of all that happened as the result of my looking through a letter-box is that of my father's voice going away from me, as all voices went from me.

After the violence of the inflammation had subsided I could just make out what was said to me by cupping my hand around my right ear.

Roper, the family doctor, formed his own opinions. The consultant he called in confirmed it.

Uncle Harold came over. He told me, "It's a great pity, Ronald. The hardest of hard luck. But with God's help you'll learn to bear it bravely. You will never hear again in your left ear. The hearing in your right is much less impaired. We must pray that in time it will improve."

I have never heard another sound in my left ear since.

Neither Dr. Roper nor the specialist could have realised, in those days, that the most grievous damage of all had been done to my eyes.

Chapter 7

WEARYBONES HILL

I was pedalling my motor-car down the avenue when I saw Daddy coming from the Parade.

"Good-oh. Daddy's home early."

I PAAP-PAAPED the horn and pedalled as fast as I could to meet him. Daddy didn't even turn his head. I PAAP-PAAPED again but he walked straight into the house. I left my motor car and ran after him. He was in the drawing room with mother.

"Daddy . . . Daddy . . . Why didn't you . . . "

"Hush," said Mummy. "Daddy's ill."

Daddy said, "I'm not. Just dog tired."

A totally strange sense of unease made me stand silent and still. I had heard them talking about Daddy's tiredness before. But not like this. I'd heard them talking above my head when I was playing. This time they seemed to be talking straight at me and yet talking as though I was not there. I watched them and listened.

"I'm all right I tell you. Don't fuss."

"I'll bring you a cup of tea and some aspirins. Then I'll send for Doctor Roper."

"Damn Roper. Tea. A hot bath. A good long sleep and I'll be right as a trivet in the morning."

"We'll see," said Mother and went to the kitchen.

Daddy suddenly clenched his fist and punched one of the sofa cushions. I was shocked. I'd been waiting for him to look at me, to speak to me. Instead, he pulled a bag of plums from his jacket pocket. He ripped open the bag. Juice dripped down his chin at the first bite.

Daddy liked bringing home little treats for us. The sight of those big red plums should have made me feel that everything was all right. But it didn't. I hesitated. Then I said, "Daddy. Can I have a plum?" I held out my hand. Daddy pushed me away from him so hard that I fell on my back. I was too amazed to cry out. He had never raised his hand to me in all my life. What was the matter? I knew I'd done nothing wrong. A child's sense of justice is not complicated and needs no summing up — no judge — no jury.

I don't remember much of what happened after that. Everything around me was confusion. Doctor Roper came and went. Uncle James. Grandma Scriven. Aunt Jess. They were all talking and rushing about. Only Aunt Jess talked to me. Then Daddy was taken to hospital.

My Grandfather Charles Scriven had four hundred-odd patents to his name when he died. His sons had inherited his engineering brains, each in different measure and degree. Caution — that prime virtue in an engineer — was second and third nature to James. My father was all for tackling a problem boldly.

War exerted a like pressure on both of them. Machines, machines, machines. Machine tools, the machines which make the machines, were a top priority. Machines which made the machines to make the guns, the shells. Plate-edge planers to trim a five-hundredth-of-an-inch the steel squares which, riveted, made the hulls of ships. Wheels, wheels, wheels for the goods trains, the moving backbone of the war machine itself.

For two years my father had been at the centre of enormous pressure and great responsibility. So had James. But his very caution was armour-plate to withstand everything flung against it.

In doing his share of keeping that machine moving, my father had for two years given everything he had to give. His brains. His energy. His stamina. He had worked with his head, with his hands, with every minute of his time and late into night after night on his drawing board and in his darkroom at home.

He had not worked quite with his whole heart. A large part was all for volunteering to fight. There was no question of my father being allowed to join up. The country could not do without men like my father. The mechanics, especially the machine-tool men, had their ranks depleted but key men were exempted.

Mother, distraught by his cracking up, reproached herself. For months she had been warning my father. She had seen at closest quarters what was happening to him. What made it worse for her was the very fact that she knew more than most wives could have done the nature of her husband's work.

A consulting engineer at twenty-two, he had taken only two years to prove himself far more than able. He'd enormously enjoyed giving my mother the clothes she loved. Taking her to the concerts which so delighted her. The little disappointments never became tiffs. If he couldn't take her to the theatre because he had to peg away at the drawing office, Mother understood why. As production on the war machines moved into top gear,

Father fitted up, in the new, larger house in Harehills Avenue, what had been a small bedroom into a work-room. There, he could use his drawing-board and draughtsman's accessory tools; and next to it, the boxroom, he made into a darkroom where he developed his blueprints. There, late night after late night, he dealt with the overspill of work which was forever mounting.

Loving, muddle-headed Gran who couldn't tell a nut from a bolt, supplied to both Father and Mother a strength which it was not in her to draw upon for herself.

James was a tower of strength.

"There is no point," he said, "in keeping on Harehills Avenue indefinitely until such time as Jack recovers. From what I have learned he will be in hospital for some considerable time."

Florence, James added, would gladly take us, but it was wartime. He, James, knew his duty, which was to shoulder Jack's responsibilities. He didn't mention that these included the extra work in the machine tool shops which must be done. Apathetic by now, unable as well as unwilling to oppose James decisions, Mother agreed to everything he suggested. "You and the boys must stay with Mother and Jess in Ellers Road. You'll be a bit cramped, but no matter. I will make the arrangements."

In all this whirligig of events I did not understand, nobody answered my questions. Mother just told me to be good and leave her alone. But why? Gran said, "Darling, mother has had too much to do and she can't stand much more from two noisy boys. Why not give Neville a ride in your motor car?"

I was baffled. There were so many things *I* wanted to

know. I asked Aunt Jess.

"What is a breakdown? What *did* Daddy break down?"

"He had a breakdown in health, darling."

What *was* a breakdown in health?

"Will they mend his breakdown in hospital?" I asked.

"Doctors and nurses are trying to make him better as soon as they can."

Much later I was to learn something of which at the time I had no clue.

An unsettled woman changes her habits. As long as I could remember there had been a time for getting up and a time for going to bed. A time for breakfast and a time for supper. Now, there were no mealtimes as there had been when father came home. Mother would sit by herself for hours looking into the drawing-room fire. I knew not to go near her. When Neville was hungry he would rush in, "Mummy. I'm starving." Then Mother would jump up and say, "Oh darling. I'm so sorry." She would make him something to eat, but not a meal. One night I felt very thirsty. I crept downstairs to the kitchen for a drink of water. Going back to the stairs I heard a noise in the drawing-room.

It was Mother and she was crying. I ran and put my arms round her and she pulled me towards her. I felt her wet cheeks against mine and started to cry too. I wanted desperately to *do* something for her "Mummy, Mummy. Don't cry. Isn't there anything I can *do* for you?"

"Nobody can do anything for me, dear. Nobody." Then she hugged me. "Yes. I've a headache. You can brush my hair."

I rushed for the hairbrush. I'd sometimes been allowed to brush her hair when Mummy was getting ready to go to the theatre. She shook down her dark brown hair. I brushed and as I brushed I tried to shine into her hair all the love I felt for her. She sat very still. When she spoke she said, "That's lovely, dear. But, oh, it's so late, it's time you were back in bed."

"You go to bed too, Mummy."

"I can't sleep. I can't sleep. I can't." She burrowed her face into her hands and started to cry in sort of great choking gulps. I threw my arms around her again. She sobbed at me, "Go away, Ronald. Go to bed."

Next day I woke to the worst bad dream of all. Gran shook me into it. "You must stay in bed for a while. Don't come down till I call you."

"Why Gran? I want to get up. I want to see Mummy."

"You can't. Doctor Roper is with her."

I felt awful. Nobody came near me for hours, yet the sun had only moved from the foot of the bed a few squares up the quilt when I heard voices. What was happening? Aunt Jess came in.

"What are they doing to Mummy? I want to see her."

"You can't just now. Nobody's doing anything to her, she is just being taken care of. Grandma and I are going to take care of you and Neville for a while. You can get dressed now."

"Where *is* Neville?"

"He's with your other grandmother. I'll take you along later, dear."

"Are they going to take Mummy to hospital to be with Daddy? I want to see her. Let me see her at once."

"Ronald. I didn't want to upset you. And it would have upset her too much to say goodbye. She's gone already."

"How long for?" I asked. "Tell me, tell me."

"Darling," said Aunt Jess. "The doctors and nurses are

going to get on with the job of *making* them both better."

"Be brave," said Aunt Florence. "If you go about looking miserable . . . . "

"And not eating properly," said Aunt Jess.

"Why, you'll make Neville upset too," said Grandma "and what good would that do?"

Aunt Jess said, "You can keep cheerful, which will help all of us to be of good heart."

James took no part in pouring soothing syrup over my distracted head. He came one morning and said "I've arranged everything."

The train from Leeds stopped at a small country station. In the shafts of an ancient four-wheeled cab a bony horse looked as though those shafts were holding him up. His Methuselah of a driver got the ramshackle contraption going, but only just.

"It smells," said Neville, jumping up and down. "I can smell straw and horse and . . . . "

"Sit down," said Uncle James.

I didn't know where we were going. Wherever it was, I didn't want to go there.

It wouldn't have been so bad if Grandma had been there, or Aunt Jess. I felt sullen and resentful. I knew what Uncle James was going to do. He was going to leave us with strangers. James jerked down the window.

"Fresh air. Nothing like the country."

I put my head out.

"Let me look too, Ron. I can see a river."

"The Wharfe," said James.

What did I care what it was called? It flowed very slowly backwards out of sight. Very straight railway lines on the right looked as though, like the road, they had been drawn with a ruler. They looked like broken chocolate. Then I saw it. Beyond the broken chocolate fields there loomed a vast bulk. Imaginative reading, well-read beyond my years in Ballantine and Henty, the unborn poet within me stirred. I saw the hill as a tremendous whale, surfacing. Cloud shadows sluiced down its side as water does when a real whale surfaces. I stared at the real hill.

The cab stopped. On the gate of the level crossing I read three words — LOW MOOR FARM.

Jolt, went the wheels. Jolt. Jolt. Jolt.

The cart track was deeply rutted. Neville gloated. "Blackberries, Ron. Tons of 'em."

The farmyard gate had been propped open. Between the kitchen door and a pump taller than herself stood a woman. Her hair was drawn back from her wrinkled forehead as though it had been almost dragged out by its roots. She was wearing a faded blue print blouse. Her long black skirt was fronted by a white apron tied as tightly behind her waist as her hair had been screwed into a bun behind her head. She was smiling.

"I'se gotten all ready, Mr. James. Make your ways in."

Neville did, in a rush. My uncle walked in. Slowly, reluctantly, I followed.

"This is Ronald, Mrs. Robinson," my uncle said. "This is Neville."

I said, deliberately politely, "How do you do?"

"Eh? Middlin'."

She gave me a bird-sharp look. She turned to James.

"If you'd like a wash, Mr. James, I'll teem a lading can o' hot water from t' hob. There's nowt but cold running water in t' scullery."

"Don't trouble yourself, Mrs. Robinson. I've washed before in cold water."

"I'se gotten a cloth laid in t'parlour. I'll fetch tea."

Neville couldn't understand her speech. I could. Fred had taught me the debased town version of broad Yorkshire. Nobody had taught me to appraise Ann's kitchen for what it was.

The flagstones had been scrubbed to Dutch cleanliness. The grain of the long dresser stood up in ridges, like hard-ribbed sand. The big kitchen range had been black-leaded until it shone as darkly as the fire-irons had been burnished bright. Concessions to comfort were few and grudging. A folded horse blanket ran the length of the long settle. One Windsor chair had been padded with felt. On the other a black-and-white cat was curled on the only cushion in the place. The only ornament was a curiously mounted silver rod with a curved handle which was tied by a knot of faded blue ribbon to a nail in the wall.

A grandfather clock which had come a long way down in the world put a face of resigned dignity on circumstances which had brought it so low. The old gentleman wore his heart, not on his sleeve, but swinging to and fro behind a pane of glass surgically set in his stomach.

Ann led us to the parlour through a stone corridor which smelled of that cleanliness which is next to ungodliness.

It was a museum in one room. The musty smell was put to rout when Ann came in with a loaded tray.

"Ham?" said my uncle.

"Eggs."

"And by Jove, kidneys." He tied a capacious table napkin behind his ears. A redoubtable trencherman, he did full justice to Mrs. Robinson's summat and nowt.

I waded in with gusto and so did Neville.

In those last awful days at home, I'd had no meals

but irregular snacks.

Here were good things galore. White bread. Brown bread. Seedy cake. Lemon curd tart cut in great wedges.

When we had all about stuffed ourselves bung full, Mrs. Robinson came in again with a great glass dish and a blue-and-white ringed jug.

"It's all I can gie ye for afters. Hazel pears, bottled last back end."

Everything was heightened for me that day. Emotional tension. The sick misery of being led into what every instinct told me was a house of bondage.

Now I let go in another direction. It was the first time I had ever tasted hazel pears, which are different, when cooked, from any other kind of pear in the world. Hazels, the small, almost nut-hard russet-skinned fruit which, like crab apples, only boys would think of eating raw off the trees.

For the rest of my life I have loved hazels, more than the jargonelle, which drops from the bough by its own weight. For me, no pear melts on the palate like a stewed hazel.

Replete, James sat down in a horsehair armchair a century old, and lit a cigar.

In the corner of the parlour I saw a cottage piano with the keyboard lid shut.

I opened it.

Mother had taught me a few simple tunes.

I began to pick out

Oh, I can wash my father's shirt,

Oh, I can wash it clean.

Oh, I can wash my father's shirt

and hang it . . . .

"Let me play. Let me." Neville made dischords play

hammer and tongs on the yellowed ivory keys.

James started from his chair as though the horsehairs had turned into wasp stings.

"Quiet," he roared.

Having seated us, he relit his cigar. Neville was sulking at the window. I went over to him.

Out of the window, I could see the great, green, shadow-sluicing whaleback of the hill.

Neville nearly split my eardrum. "Look at that. There. There."

In a scruffy little garden just outside the window, strutted beauty incarnate. I had seen pictures of peacocks. The hundred-eyed, thousand-jewelled splendours of this princely creature set my astonished imagination back on its heels.

Even as my eyes took in the sight, the peacock shawled the shimmering glory of his train and flew up onto the ridge-roof of a barn. He flung back his crested head and screamed.

The sound was like that of a lost soul in limbo, crying out for either heaven or hell, one could not tell which.

As though summoned by the unearthly sound, Mrs. Robinson came in.

"That's Pharaoh, my peacock. Allus gie's me warnin'. Weather'll change in a two-three days I reckon."

When we set off up the cart-track, James carried a knapsack slung over his back. It bulged with a Low Moor ham and other good things of Mrs. Robinson's making. Neville, his chubby legs clasping James' neck, rested his bum on the knapsack.

"Not too far for your young legs, Ronald. Now you've had a tasting sample of Mrs. Robinson's excellent fare, you'll know why I brought you here. What lucky boys you're going to be. You'll live like fighting cocks on the sort of fare townsfolk like me only dream about."

"It was scrumptious," said Neville.

"It was," I said.

"Mr. and Mrs. Robinson are good, honest, kindly warm-hearted Yorkshire folk. I congratulate myself on having found them." Said Uncle.

When we reached the inside gate of the level-crossing he told me, "You must look after your young brother. If ever you have occasion to use this crossing, make absolutely sure no train is coming."

"There's a train coming now, Uncle. I can hear it," said Neville.

I couldn't. But I could see the dropped signal arm.

My uncle swung Neville down. I climbed the gate. Soon even my deaf ear told me that the engine was a powerful one. The locomotive's seven-foot coupled driving wheels clanked, its plume of white steam condensed on coach after coach. I counted fourteen of them. At the windows, I could see a blurred, rippling line of faces. And each coach was marked by a huge red cross.

"War wounded," said Uncle. "Poor devils."

That was the first week of September 1916. On the first of July, 20,000 British soldiers had been killed on the Somme. Few and lucky were the wounded who came back to Blighty. This batch was singing.

"Pack up your troubles in your old kit-bag and smile, smile, smile."

My Uncle said, as the last coach passed, "Well, we part company here. Be good, both of you. Mrs. Robinson will take the place of your mother, Ronald."

79

"She won't. Nobody will ever take the place of my mother." I burst out.

James felt in his pocket. "There, there, my boy. You'll settle down."

He pressed two coins into my hand, one into Neville's.

We watched him cross, close the far gate, turn, wave and stride away.

It was the last time I was to see one of my own for the duration of our stay at Low Moor.

Mrs. Robinson was waiting for us. "Did yer Uncle gie ye owt? Turn out yer pockets."

I desperately wanted some comfort, any kind of comfort. I couldn't think what to say so I mumbled. "I want to buy some sweets."

"Sweets? There's no shop 'ere. Yer'll none need onny brass at Low Moor. Put these in t' pig bank."

She slotted in the coins and put the piggy-bank on the high mantelshelf.

Neville said "Come on Ron. We'll go out and play."

"That yer won't. Tha've none cum 'ere t' play. Off to bed wi'ye. Ye'se gettin' up early ti-morn."

After we'd said our prayers and Mrs. Robinson, who hadn't listened to them, had gone, there was enough daylight left for me to look about our new, forbidding bedroom.

On the wall at the foot of the bed was a picture. The picture of an awful eye. It glared horribly. THOU, GOD, SEEST ME.

The bed was a goosefeather one. Behind my head the long bolster was as hard as the bed was soft. The feel of the sheets was coarse. They had the pungent smell of carbolic soap and were chill and stiff.

Neville, like a small animal seeking warmth, snuggled against me.

"Get up. We've got to say our prayers."

He snuggled closer.

"We've said our prayers."

"Get out of bed. We're going to say them properly."

Kneeling in our nightshirts on the cold linoleum floor, we put our palms together, our prayers ending " . . . . Please, God, please make Mummy and Daddy better soon."

The warmth of his small body in my arms and my own body-heat slowly distilled from the goosefeather bed the opiate of sleep. I was shaken back to consciousness by Mrs. Robinson. "I'se shouted three times . . . I'll knock wi't broomhead on't ceiling t'morn. Get thi's brother dressed, sharp. T' breakfast's ready."

In the kitchen, sitting in the chair with the hard flat pad was a man who was the size and shape of a beer barrel, with long arms and short legs. He wore a cloth cap which might once have been grey. From ear to ear a reddish brown beard, neatly enough clipped, stretched in a semicircle about an inch in thickness. Old-fashioned people called this style a Newgate fringe.

Joe Robinson was old fashioned enough to have shambled out of the pages of *Bleak House*. He gave the two of us an incurious look and went on eating.

"Sit thissens on t' settle," said Mrs. Robinson.

"Theer." She placed before each of us a bowl and a spoon.

"Oatmeal porridge. If tha wants sugar tha's gettin' none. Tha can 'ave as much salt as tha' likes."

She poured milk over the porridge.

At home, I'd enjoyed criss-crossing my porridge with golden syrup. I tasted. The first spoonful was so hot that I didn't notice the taste. I breathed in to cool my mouth and that made the taste of the second spoonful get a real grip on my palate. The stuff was revolting. It was full of podge lumps. I couldn't stand slimey podge lumps.

Mrs. Robinson's sharp eye was on me. I bit. The lump was dry and gritty inside. I pushed away the bowl.

"I don't like this porridge, Mrs. Robinson."

"It's none what tha likes," said Mrs. Robinson. "It's what tha's gettin'."

"I can't eat it, Mrs. Robinson. Truly."

Mrs. Robinson picked up the bowl. She put it on the high mantle-shelf beside the piggy-bank and put a plate on top.

"When tha wants it, tha can ask for it. Tha'll get nowt else till tha diz."

Hunger sauce can disguise even the taste of podge lumps.

Neville ate enough of the revolting stuff to satisfy himself and — in a far different sense — Mrs. Robinson.

I had pride. So had Mrs. Robinson. She made me sit at table not only when breakfast was on it but at dinner time and supper time. Dinner looked good and smelt better and supper spread a different home-made jam on its oven cake every evening.

Mrs. Robinson smacked Neville' slice of strawberry jam to the floor the first time he tried to pass it to me on the sly.

"Tha can clean that up an' all," she told him.

I had pride. So had Mrs. Robinson. It took her three days to break my pride.

All she said when I did ask was, "Tha mun wait till I boils it up."

Joe Robinson slapped what, if his body really had been a beer barrel, would have been the bung. "Nowt like oatmeal porridge," he guffawed. "Look what it's done fer me."

My surrender had been hastened by the pig-bucket. Every morning when Joe had gone I had to carry a pail of kitchen scraps to the pig-sty. Emma, the large white Yorkshire sow, was bloatedly in pig. The last two days before I ran up the white flag I did her out of some potato-peelings and a piece of pastry crust.

In the farmyard the fresh air my uncle James had praised so highly was freshened still more by Emma and by the matched plough-horses, Prince and Diamond, by hay maturing in the barn, and most of all by the dunghill.

The cock who lorded it and his White Wyandotte concubines flew at me. "Give 'im a bit o' boot-toe, lad," Joe shouted.

Laconic out of doors, at home Joe hadn't word for the cat. He was a slow relentless worker. Villagers called him 'Slow Joe'. Like the good farmer he was, he had an eye for all his animals. Only under stress of hay or corn harvesting did he every work any of them beyond what he judged was their capacity. He dosed them, when out of sorts, with remedies of primitive simplicity. Bartholomew on *Farriery* was his bible. I did not know that Slow Joe had his eye on me, a young animal out of sorts.

He never interfered with matters he considered his wife's concern, any more than she would have poked her nose into what was his business, such as paring the hooves of sheep with a horn-handled knife and then treating them with Stockholm tar.

He was illiterate — all but. Ann Robinson did what little writing on farm business had to be done. All this, of course, I was to learn, painfully. In the beginning, if he had seen me helping myself from Emma's pig bucket he kept his own counsel, at which he was a capital hand. He wanted me hale and strong for a sound reason. In the dawn age of farming, Joe managed Low Moor, including the eighty acres of the Rasser, the largest field for many miles around, with the help of one man, Edgar Artackle.

A sturdily built, nine-year-old boy would augment his labour force and what was more demand no wages.

Slow Joe eyed Neville as a working animal no more than he would have thought of a foal in terms of harnessing it to a cart. Neville was his wife's concern. She worked as hard as Joe did. Neville could and had to lighten her burden by being at her beck and call in the kitchen, the scullery and the dairy.

The black and white cattle dog, Laddie, was Slow Joe's shadow. Like all farmers who have to handle bulls he never went abroad without his stout ashplant. I was frightened when I saw him slash it crack across the knee-caps of a bull. I thought the bull would turn on him but it only shook its great head and backed away. Joe was a dab hand at knocking over a rabbit with that ashplant, hurled with all the power of his arm.

My return to a state of grace and favour in Ann's eyes I celebrated at dinner time.

Rabbit pie, baked by Ann under a crust which glued its lips to the dish with its own gravy. No better dish to feast on than I revelled in that dinner time in Ann's kitchen.

"Tha can gie Joe a hand wi' t' muckin' out," said Mrs. Robinson. "Ee's taken t' pig bucket across t' yard. And think on tha brings it back."

The barrow was caked with muck. Muck slopped into

the brick channels dividing the stalls where the cows were chained. Mr. Robinson, his milking cap at the back of his head, was milking. Hard as oak, his fingers rhythmically stripped each teat of the udder, squirting milk into the can, before shifting himself and his three-legged stool to the next stall.

In the wake of his milky way I shovelled the muck into the barrow, wheeled it out, tipped it on to the midden and wheeled back the barrow to muck out some more.

Edgar Artackle, Joe's day labourer, gave me a hint. An East-Riding man, his speech had a musical softness, more pleasing to my ear than the curt harshness of the West Riding.

Dress Edgar in Viking gear, clap a horned helmet on his head and tell him to keep his trap shut — he could have gone aboard any longship unchallenged.

"Hold t'shovel low doon wi' thi' left hand, lad. Thoo'll lift it easier."

Mucking out was one of Edgar's hundred-odd jobs. As I became more useful to Joe, however, Edgar made time to ease the yoke on my young shoulders with many a practical tip.

My grace and favour with Ann was short-lived. One dinner time I took into the kitchen a long, lovely tail-plume Pharaoh had moulted. Ann boxed my ears.

"I'll learn thi to bring t' evil eye int' t' house," she said.

How she reconciled this old pagan superstition with keeping the peacock itself puzzled my nine-year-old wits.

Puzzled though I was by that conundrum, my next mishap utterly confounded me. A bit of larking about with Neville before bedtime Ann tolerated, provided she was satisfied that we'd done the washing up properly. In a last romp, I accidentally knocked the curious silver rod from its nail on the wall. As I stooped to pick it up, Ann fell on me in a fury. It was the more frightening because she set about me in silence.

In bed, Neville tried to comfort me. My hard, dry sobs were not to be comforted. To be so severely punished for no crime at all seemed to me injustice beyond reason.

When I was mucking out next day, Edgar came up to me.

"Joe tell't me thoo fell foul of Ann last neet." He laid a hand on my shoulder.

"Thoos none t' first lad shoos thrashed. Thoo thinks shoos hard on thee. Shoo were so hard on her own son, John, that when he war thirteen he ran away to sea sooner nor put up wi her. What brought it to a head were when John broke his bicycle. Shoo told Joe to gie him a belting for that an' he did, not arf. Yon thing shoos hung on t' kitchen wall wor t' lad's front brake. Aye. Brake o' his bike's all shoo's gotten to remember him by. Folks in't village 'as called 'er 'Iron Ann' ever sin'."

So that was why Ann had polished a memory every Saturday night and I'd thought it was something in silver. Iron Ann? Iron Ann. The village was dead right.

The corn cut, the two men worked to clear the twenty-acre home field. Ann worked beside me tieing the sheaves with hairy twine.

The fine weather held. We worked on until the stooks were set up. The field was beautiful. It looked as though it lifted to heaven, hands clasped together in prayers of thanksgiving for harvest home.

"That's last on't," said Joe. "Nowt to do but make

t' Corn Dolly."

I watched Joe making the corn dolly. He lashed
together the last two sheaves. He shaped the dolly's
head, her arm and legs. Joe let me help him to carry her
into a corner of the field.

In man's dim past he had got it into his head that a
sacrifice at the end of the harvest would remind the
corn goddess to grow green grass and young green corn
again. I didn't know that then, and when I asked Joe all
he said was "We allus makes 'em."

On Sunday night, Iron Ann said, "All t' lads that's
been helpin' to get t' harvest in is goin' back to school
ti'morn. Tha's goin' an' all. Sam Longster fro' t' next
farm'll tak' thi."

"Goody," said Neville, "And me."

"Thee? Tha's too young."

The harvest moon had risen high over Wearybones
Hill. The moonlight shone on the linoleum. My feet
felt as though they were wading through a pool of silver.
I looked out of the window at the huge hill. My great
whale.

I talked to him sometimes. Somewhere a long way
over his back was home.

There was a lovely warm, earthy smell from the stable.

School tomorrow. I hugged myself. School. No Iron
Ann all day long.

Chapter 8

DOMINIE DOBSON

Before Ann could knock with her broom on freedom day, I was up and downstairs. "Tha can tak t' pig-bucket across t' yard," said Ann.

"Nah then," she said when I went back, "Off wi' them clothes. I'se putten thi new ones i' thi bedroom."

Neville's sleep had been rubbed out of his eyes when he saw my new clothes. I stared at them aghast. I put them on. The thick union shirt was a size too big. The breeches sagged. The sleeves of the jacket came down to my fingers. The pair of leather leggings which looked like drainpipes, felt rigid, like drainpipes, and to underscore indignity, clogs.

"Ann's shouting," said Neville. "Buck up. Oh Ron, you look awful."

Another voice from downstairs shouted as I stumbled into the kitchen.

"I'se 'ere, Mrs. Robi'son." Sam Longster barged in, cap in hand.

Ann handed me the only item of my new outfit which I didn't hate at sight. A brand-new school satchel.

"I'se putten thi dinner in t'. 'Ere's thi cap."

I crammed the grey horror on my head.

Sam watched me curiously as, rocking on the unaccustomed clogs, I walked beside him up the cart-track.

He said nothing, which was what Sam mostly said.

From the level crossing it was a mild-and-a-half to the top of Rigton Hill, the squat, ungainly, dumpier brother of Wearybones.

The clog irons skidded on the road. Three-quarters of the way up, Sam, out of his few words, used two of them. He pointed and said "Yon's schooil."

School was a grim, chunky building built of the same local stone as the square tower of North Rigton church, its neighbour, and Low Moor farm.

Boys were kicking a football about in the yard. A man whose presence was AUTHORITY personified stood in the doorway. He held up a big shiny bell by its handle and suddenly made it go CLANG CLANG CLANG. The boys filed past us into the school.

"I'se fetched 'im, sir," said Sam.

Dominie Dobson, the Schoolmaster, took me aside. "How badly is your hearing affected, Ronald?"

"I can hear you, sir."

"H'mm. Come with me."

The master's desk was on a dais. He put me bang in the middle of the front row within a foot of his own platform. For the whole of my time at North Rigton school it was his habit to stand over me and make sure that I heard what he said. If I could hear him, the rest could.

When the bell went for dinner break, boys who lived in the village scampered off to their homes. Those who, like me, lived too far away ate whatever they'd brought with them.

"What's Ann Robi'son gied thee?"

I rummaged my satchel.

"Cowd rice pud, eh?" said Sam. "Thowt it 'ud be summat o't sort."

He took the tin from me and put it on top of the school stove. Now the master had gone, the boys crowded round me.

"What's yer name? Scriven. A right daft name."

"Where didsta live afore tha comed t' Low Moor?"

"Cansta fight?"

"Come on, show us."

"Leave him be," said Sam Longster, "or I'll bash thee."

I was bewildered. When Sam had called for me all I could think of at first was that I was going to get away from Iron Ann. Once I'd got away, the nearer we came to Rigton school, the more I was convinced that I'd make friends with the boys. And here they were, crowding round me, jeering at me, mocking my deafness, hustling me, tormenting me because I was a stranger and didn't speak broad Yorkshire as they did.

I could understand what they said all right. They were shouting. Fred had taught me the West Riding form of dialect.

One of them pushed at me. I lashed out.

In an instant we were rolling over each other on the playground, fighting with our fists and our feet.

"Give it 'im Sid," they yelled.

The two of us were suddenly hoisted to our feet by the scruff of our necks. Dominie Dobson said "That's enough you two. Now shake hands."

Walking at Sam's side across the valley, Sam said "Tha' did weal."

I felt happy.

It was good to be told I'd held my own in my new school. Deep inside, I knew that I would have to do that wherever I went.

Before we reached Low Moor, Sam said "I'll be seein' thi' t'morn. I'se off 'ome."

Low Moor was all that I could call home. I didn't want to go there. It wasn't my home but Iron Ann's.

"So tha's back," she said. "Sit thee at t'table."

"It's Yorkshire pud wi' rabbit an' onion gravy. I've had mine," shouted Neville.

"Then it's ham and eggs. Scrumptious."

Ann planked the Yorkshire pudding in front of me. "Them as eats most pud," she said "gets most meat."

I didn't know then this was an old dodge to make children stuff themselves so full of pudding that they had scarcely any room left for the meat.

In bed, Neville peppered my ear with questions.

"Ron, what was school like? Ron, did you like it? Ron, what sort of games do they play at school?"

Dominie Dobson assessed my strengths and weaknesses. He put a prompt finger on both. The twice-times table he ground into me methodically. He discovered within a week that I was a good reader. He set me homework to my joyous liking.

The first time I spread my exercise book on the table after my evening meal, Ann said "Tha goes t' schooil t' be schooild. Tha comes 'ome to mak' thissen useful. Put them books away."

When I had to explain why I hadn't done my homework to Mr. Dobson, he gave me a sealed letter to give to Ann.

She read the letter but she sent back no reply.

Next day Mr. Dobson set me some more written questions. They troubled me all the way down Rigton Hill. How could I possibly disobey Mr. Dobson? How could I possibly disobey Ann?

"Get on wi' thi 'omework. Tha's to do what Mr. Dobson tells thi."

I made a guess that this was the first time for many a year Iron Ann had come against an authority stronger than her own.

I knew from things he said that Edgar had known Iron Ann for a long time. I learned a lot of things about her from him.

I knew Ann never went to church. When had she time to go? It was Edgar who told me that Ann had been taught when she was young to remember the Sabbath day, to keep it holy. He reckoned she'd kept it holy all her married life. That's to say, he said, she works harder in the house and the dairy on Saturdays and does no more on Sunday than she has to. And what was more, she saw to it that Joe did as little as he had to about the farm.

Saturday night, Edgar said, was Joe's night. "Thoo knows 'e's nivver a word for t' cat at home. Noo. I'll cap thee. On Saturdays in t' Square an' Compass Joe's life an' soul o' t' tap, wi' t' tales 'ee tells and by gow, can he sup his ale."

When Neville and I had washed up, Ann put on her steel-rimmed specs and sat down to read the Bible. The nights were drawing in. Its wick trimmed, she lit her oil lamp. I liked that lamp. It had a fat, green glass belly and a clear glass funnel. I watched her lips move slowly as she read.

Ann's Bible had a great brass clasp. Sometimes she frowned as she read. I knew it wasn't the print that was bothering her. That was big and black. She puckered her forehead. I watched both Ann and the clock. She'd sent Neville to bed when she'd lit the lamp. When would she send me? I didn't want to leave the warm kitchen.

What *was* Ann looking for in the Bible? I'd often seen her ferreting about in her workbox trying to find a needle or a reel of cotton, or she'd mislaid her thimble. She seemed to be doing the same sort of thing with the Bible. She kept on opening it, reading a bit and shutting it and opening it again in another place. I could tell she didn't want to give it up as a bad job and get on with darning one of our socks or mending one of Joe's jackets. She'd be sending me to bed soon. I looked at the clock, again. When I looked at Ann she said "Fetch mi workbox. Tha can read t' Good Book to me while I'se mendin'."

"Where shall I read, please?"

Ann frowned more deeply. What was puzzling her now? I got it. She didn't know herself. She bit off the end of a thread.

"Oppen it anywhere."

The Bible fell open at 11 Chronicles.

"Where's thi thumb restin'?"

"On verse 13, chapter 31."

"Read it," she said.

"'Know ye not what I and my father have done unto all the people of other lands? Were the gods of the nations of those lands and ways able to deliver their lands out of mine hands?'"

Oh, how boring the Bible was. Ann said "Nowt theere. Oppen t' Good Book again, same as before an' read."

"Two Kings. Chapter 9. It's verse 20. 'And the watchman told, saying, He came even unto them, and cometh not again: and the driving is like the driving of Jehu, the son of Nimshi; for he driveth furiously.'"

I liked that. I could see Jehu driving furiously, like Isaac Brogden driving his milk float like mad down Rigton Hill.

I wanted to know what Jehu was driving so I looked at Ann and saw she was thinking it over. I skipped up the page and there it was. And, Jehu rode a chariot. I could read with my eyes faster than Ann could.

"Try somewheer else."

I opened the Bible again. "Proverbs. Chapter 17. Verse 25. 'A foolish son is a grief to his father, and bitterness to her that bore him.'"

"Shut t' book," said Ann, sharply. She looked at John's bicycle brake on the wall. She muttered: "Aye. Foolish. That's what 'e were."

I didn't wait for her to tell me to go to bed.

Like all the other boys, I had to put up with whatever weather autumn sent as I trudged the mile-and-a-half up Rigton Hill, the mile-and-a-half down.

Our greatcoats steamed the classroom windows, the stove glowed heating up my tin of cold rice pud or toasting the dog biscuits Alan and I often crunched for afters.

Alan Church had been a friend from the day of my first scrap. Open-hearted, open-handed, his generosity embarrassed me. His satchel was stuffed with apple pie and other good things. What could I offer in return? Hotted-up rice pud.

Even worse was my poverty when it came to sharing sweets, which Yorkshire boys called spice. I had none to share and so refused when other boys offered me aniseed balls or a suck of their gob-stoppers.

Alan said "Go on, have some. Some on 'em seys Ann

Robi'son t'meanest woman i' Wharfedale."

Alan came from a good home. Many a lad didn't. Sons of day labourers often took to school no more than a scraping of bread and dripping. A lot depended on whether or not the farmers their fathers worked for were mean or not, well-to-do or little better off than their labourers.

The Dominie kept me pegging away at the three R's.

On Saturdays, I was not the only one who was found plenty to do. Nearly all my schoolfellows had to work on the land whenever they could.

Harvest long over, the back-end was for ploughing, sowing, hedging and ditching and all the odd jobs that had to be tackled with the scantiest of manpower.

The war, they said, was going badly.

Parker, whose farm was on the other side of Low Moor from Sam Longster, had a German prisoner of war working for him. They said he was a Bavarian and a good worker.

"Nobbut t' rest on 'em were like 'im," said Edgar, "they'd do awreet."

One of my Saturday jobs was to lend a hand with whitewashing Emma's sty. Joe trundled a tub to the low brick wall of the sty and brewed the whitewash. He handed me the sawn-off chunk of an old broom handle and said, "Stir it. Ah's off t' t' loft t' cut some chaff."

Neville, who adored Emma, was all for bagging the job for himself. I climbed the small gate and on to the wall of the sty.

Emma lay on her side of the straw Joe had cleared out of her sty. She was snoring contentedly in the late October sunshine.

A wonderful idea came to me. I'd give Emma a coat of whitewash. The flat brush lay beside the whitewash tub. "Come on, Nev. Emma's too hot with all those piglings in her tummy. Let's cool her down." At the first slosh, Emma opened her pink eyes and heaved with pleasure. Slosh, slosh. She was lovely to whitewash. My enthusiasm, aided and abetted by whoops from Neville, increased. Flicks of whitewash flew like soap suds. The wall of the sty was spattered. Neville's clothes were splashed. Mine were daubed.

Slow Joe's roar of rage so startled Neville that he lost his balance and fell backwards into the tub.

Next Saturday Ann said "Joe's gotten a surprise for thee. It's in t' barn."

"Can I see what it is?"

"Aye," said Ann.

On the threshing floor was my motor car.

My beautiful, beautiful motor car. Bodywork had been ripped away. The steering wheel had gone. The bonnet, with real glass in the headlamps, was no longer there. Nor the pedals. The strong, rubber-tyred wheels were still there. The mudguards gone. A huge soapbox replaced front and back seats. A long loop of clothes line had been lashed to the front bumper.

"I reckon that's capped thee," said Joe. "A farmer can turn 'is 'and to owt. I'se made thee a champion cart fer t' gatherin' t' kindlin' from t' 'edge bottoms."

If I could have bashed Joe as he had bashed my beautiful, beautiful motor car, I would have done.

Afterwards I remembered that one day shortly after Uncle James had left us at Low Moor the carrier's cart had brought a big packing case which Joe had stored in the barn. Uncle James must have sent it for me all those months ago.

How dare these people do such a dreadful thing? But then how could I have understood that what had been done was not, nor intended to be, another punishment for whitewashing Emma. In Joe's eyes, he had done me a good turn by making it easier for me to collect sticks for lighting the fire.

Neville cried.

I was sick beyond tears.

"When tha's filled thi new kindlin' box," said Ann "Teem it in t' wood shed. I want yon shed filled afore winter sets in."

One morning Dominie Dobson told us that there was to be a school treat to celebrate breaking up. Everyone would be expected to bring food parcels to the feast. I was horrified. Take a tin of cold rice pud? Not likely. Only one thing for it, I told Neville. On Saturday I'd go to our hidey-hole at the back of the barn and keep out of sight all day.

I was putting on my school cap preparatory to setting off up the cart track then dodging back to the barn, when Ann said "I'se gittin thi parcel for t' schooil treat. It's summat an' nowt but it'll 'ave t' do." She handed me my satchel. It was a lot heavier than usual.

"I'll see thi off," said Ann and stood between the kitchen door and the pump as she had done on that first meeting between us. Sick at heart I trudged off, then I brightened as a plan occurred to me. I could fling the rice pud and the lumps of fat bacon or whatever other shameful things she had added over the hedge on Rigton Hill and make myself scarce for the day.

Sam Longster overtook me before I'd a chance to carry out this master-stroke. For Sam, he was loquacious.

"I'se gotten ivverything mi mum could think on. What's Ann Robinson gied thee?"

"Summat an' nowt," I groaned.

Sam gave me a startled look. It was the first time he

had ever heard me talk Yorkshire.

In rough high spirits, others joined us and I was swept up with them.

Balloons and festoons of home-made paper streamers and lanterns made the bare winter schoolroom cheerful. Cathie Dobson, the Dominie's daughter, collected everyone's parcels and piled them on the hall table. We were all in love with Cathie. I didn't look at her as I handed over Ann's miserable offering.

Carols, a crib tableau and a mumming play with the dragon, the doctor and Little Daivy Doubt with shirt tails hanging out. I joined in with everything.

The nearer it came to the dreaded time of shame, the worse I felt. The moment came. "Open your parcels," Cathie Dobson called. Ann had packed two dozen cold ham sandwiches, a dozen of strawberry jam. A baked spice loaf, two bottles of hazel pears. A cold roast chicken.

Prize of prizes, as far as the organisers of the feast were concerned, a whole pound of tea and two of sugar. In such a time of shortages, how had she managed the tea and sugar? Any farmer's wife able to swap butter, eggs and cream could have as much tea and sugar as she wanted. I'd seen Ann doing her swaps. Not for nothing was Pharaoh the symbol of Iron Ann's pride

All she said when I tried to thank her was "Didsta think I were goin' t' let Rigton folk look down theer noses at m'?"

I paid my whack of gratitude by extra hard work.

Two days before Christmas Joe took me to the barn. On the threshing floor a sack, loosely tied with harvest twine. In it he had shovelled a store of wheat ears. He handed me a flail. A short thick length of oak, hinged to a long length of ash pole.

"Thi sees yon sack? Bray it wi' t' stick."

It was harder work than turning the copperbanded oak barrel of the churn.

I brayed away all morning. Once or twice Ann came in. She rubbed the wheat between her finger and thumb. "Go on brayin'," she said.

What was I braying it for, I asked Ann. "Tha'll find out soon enough."

I bashed and mashed the grains of wheat until the kernels burst and the stuff became all creamy. Then Ann told me to carry it into the kitchen. I watched her put the wheat into a great iron cooking pot. She poured two pints of cream over it.

"What are you doing?" I asked.

"Creeding it. I'se leaving it to soak overnight. Now off to bed wi' thee."

After breakfast, she added currants, sultanas, muscatels, sticks of cinnamon and root ginger to the mess. She sent Neville to fetch a tub of allspice and goodness knows what else. Then she set the pot on a hook over the fire.

"Stir it," she told me, "and keep on stirrin' it."

With her biggest wooden spoon and Ann's eyes on me, I stirred all morning.

Christmas morning came. Without hope that Santa Claus would come, I had hung up our stockings.

Neville, who was certain that Father Christmas would come, wasn't as surprised as I was to find that he had.

We emptied the stockings. Two oranges. Two apples and a handful of cob nuts each.

"Oh, look, Ron. A teddy bear."

He hugged the little bear tightly in his arms. I remembered that bear. Daddy had bought it for him and I saw that Neville had forgotten his own toy. We had never had any toys at Low Moor.

I turned away. Then I saw a wrapped parcel. My gun mules. The gun mules which had been Daddy's last present the Christmas I got my motor car. I had not cried over what Joe had done to my beautiful, beautiful motor car. I cried over my gun mules.

We went downstairs.

"Sit thi down," said Ann. "Tha's goin' ta get a taste of what we's been makin'. Frummity."

She ladled the stuff, piping hot, into bowls and poured thick yellow cream over.

Ann always ate her breakfast by herself while Joe was milking. Today we all sat together.

"Tha can et as much as tha wants."

Frummity? I tasted it. I closed my eyes. I'd never dreamed anything could taste so marvellous. Later on manners told me I ought to say thank you to Ann. But for what? I thought it over while Neville and I washed up. Ann hadn't given us any presents at all. She'd only given us back our own toys. I wasn't going to thank her for anything. Instead, I asked "Please can I play with my gun mules?"

"Not in t' kitchen. I'se over much to do, wi t' cookin'. Christmas is t' same as Sabbath day."

I thought she was going to refuse. "Tha's nowt to do, so tha can play in t' barn."

I was glad not to see the goose go into the oven. The night Joe had killed her, I'd been as interested as Neville to watch him. Joe had got the stubble-fatted bird between his short legs, reached his horn-handled clasp knife from his back pocket, bent her neck downwards by the beak and cut her head open at the top. The spouting blood made Neville yell with glee. The sight had made me suddenly rush out of the shed.

After dinner, Joe in his Windsor chair, a pint china pot of mulled ale with a crab-apple hissing in it, drank, head-nodded, dozed and nearly nodded himself off the chair, among the fire irons.

For a while, Ann, having chased Tibby from her cushion, had a catnap too.

Neville was curled up asleep on the rag-rug. The green grass-bellied oil-lamp, wick trimmed and lit, the red window-blind drawn down like the short dusk. Grandfather clock, his dignity enhanced by his patience, counted time. There were two splashes of light against the red blind: Ann's last of the year's white roses.

I watched one of the year's last flies crawl on the wall above the nail-knotted silver of John's bicycle brake. I looked at it and wondered. Had he been in his mother's thoughts this Christmas? I thought: John should have been here. Not me. The kitchen, so quiet, so unwontedly peaceful.

Suddenly my eyes filled with desolate tears. I knew where I should have been. With Neville, on a Christmas day full of the happiness of being with Daddy and Mummy in our own home.

Chapter 9

THE SNOWS OF WINTER

In the New Year the land had tightened its belt. It was
in poor heart. By winter 1917, corn, livestock and
vegetables had been squeezed out of it by three years of
war. Manpower had been thinned. Reserves of fodder
had dwindled. Nature's power of replenishing them had
not come to a stop but her ability to do so had been
drastically foreshortened by the slow, almost impercep-
tible revolution of her own wheel of the seasons.

The times were lean like Edgar Artackle. But those who
worked on the land, if they had no reserves of fat, could,
unlike townsfolk, still live on some of that of the land.
Not for nothing.

"Sitha," Edgar said and showed me the poacher's
pocket in the lining of his jacket.

"Dip thi 'and in."

There was the soft, limp, still warm body of a bird and
two handfuls of nuts.

"It's a good man what can shoot a snipe," said Edgar,
"but thoo can trap one if thoo knows how. I found a
squirrel's 'oard o' nuts when I ganned to look fer t' trap.

Squirrels 're daft. They forget where they've putten half on 'em. Gie Neville some on 'em. Hazels, an' a few cobs."

In the cold winter months my liking for the East Riding man warmed into friendship. He was as hard a worker as Slow Joe, but Edgar always managed to find time to talk to me, when, as often happened at week ends, we worked together.

As January slowly drew away from the shortest day it wasn't at the week ends only that our working companionship, like the daylight, became stronger. The snows of winter kept me from school and Joe from the plough stilts.

"Snow's a champion blanket," said Edgar. "It's a reet good job t' back-end gied us t' chance to sow as much as we did. Come Candlemas I sal' know what kind o' a spring we's in fer. As t' weather is on Candlemas day, so will t' rest o' winter be."

Candlemas, the second of February brought harder weather. The sheep had been brought up from the Rasser and folded in the home field.

Ann had a new part-time job. Three or four lambs rejected by their ewes or made motherless by Old Bloody Beak, the carrion crow who pecks out the eyes of disabled sheep, were brought into the kitchen for her to bring up. Her hard hands were gentle with them.

If February was bleak, March came roaring in true to his lion's form. We were all having our elevenses and Edgar, finishing his pint of strong tea, sighed with satisfaction.

"I sal be reet glad to see t' spring. Thoo knows shoo's come when thoo can cover five daisies wi' one foot."

"Spring," said Ann. "Tha's made me think on. Time to purify thi blood." She went into the larder and returned with a jar and a large spoon. "Nowt like brimstun' an' tracle. Oppen thi gob."

The mixture of black molasses and sulphur didn't look as nasty as it sounded or taste as devilish. It soon made me helter-skelter through out to the earth-closet.

It had been a long-drawn spring. Now the weather began to settle. By mid-June it had almost made up its fickle mind.

One night when I came back from school Ann said, "Theers thi tea. Tha's none goin' t' schooil t' morn."

"I think we're going to dip the sheep tomorrow, Ron," said Neville.

"Had thi tongue. Tha knows nowt."

Neville rushed into the yard the better to hold his tongue.

Slow Joe was watching the clouds as though weighing up whether to dip them or the sheep in the morning. "Weather's reet," he decided.

Very early next morning we set off for the Rasser. The hedges were mist-wet, wild and wild-rosed. Cuckoo-spit clotted the grass of the Rasser. The sun, mopping the few clouds from his brow, drank the dew from the grass and the brook.

Edgar followed us down, Diamond was in the cart shafts and Neville rode triumphantly on his withers.

The cart was piled high with hurdles and ashpoles and something lumpy draped by sacks.

The sheep-dip was at the far end of the Rasser. The banks of the brook had been man-widened to make a pool four feet deep. Farther upstream our bank of the brook shelved.

Edgar and Joe set up hurdles to pen the sheep. Across the brook at the shallow end they slung ashpoles from which a wire-netting curtain was hung. A similar contraption of ashpoles and wire-netting was built at the deep end.

Laddie, who had lain in the shadow of his cart, knew his job. He needed no whistle from Joe to give him his orders. He was off, a black and white streak. Full of excitement I ran after him and Neville valiantly made after me.

"Tha' can save thi breath," yelled Joe. "Tha'll need it."

We both needed it and so did Edgar in the next hour. The sheep heavy with their winter fleece tried to outpace their lambs in making silly forays to escape. I tried to head off a group of stragglers, Neville's chubby legs did their best to head off another. The midday sun was nearing its zenith before we had the last of them penned. Then the fun really began.

Joe singled out the bellwether and booted her into the dip at the deep end. Whooping, I climbed on top of the ashpoles. A diamond-glittering shower of spray shot over me. The bellwether's grey fleece floated outwards and upwards. The rest of the sheep followed her as they were let out in batches by Edgar. The baa-ing and the bleating made a merry chorus to this Rite of Spring.

Greasy scum from the sheep-dip disinfectant filmed the pool. The scum became thicker and thicker as Joe, with the prongs of a pitchfork, forced the heads of the sheep under water. One by one they were ducked and tubbed. As each was released it floundered up the shelving bank only to find itself in the largest pen of all.

Then, bleating for their mothers, as though they had been born that day, the lambs were dealt with. Instead of using a pitchfork, Joe humped into the dip and bodily dipped the youngsters.

It was hard work. Shower after shower had drenched

me and the hot sun dried my clothes to be drenched
again. I was hoarse from shouting. Deliriously happy.
Neville was wetter than me and as blissful.

Last of all, Joe went to the cart and brought back
his milking cap. That too he tossed into the pool to
get its annual wash.

Unobserved, Ann had come down. She had unwrapped
the lumpy object from under the sacks. A four-gallon
cask of nettle beer. We flung ourselves on the happy
grass.

Neville and I, gloved and grumpy, had picked the
nettle tops to be rewarded now with long, long drinks
as paradisial as Harry Holgate's stone ginger beer.

Oven-cake baked by Ann, butter churned by her
labour saving device, me, made with the home-cured
ham sandwiches fit to be bitten into by the gods we
felt like. I munched and munched whilst the sun in
glory might well have envied me.

The sun in glory, however, was a workman too. He
had the fleeces to dry. Exhausted by their terror, done
with their ordeal by water, they were content to let the
sun get on with the job.

We, like the hill, rested our weary bones. No more
pressure of hard work to make them wearier. Joe, hard,
relentless driver as he was, knew that. Was he totally
insensitive to the beauty he had, in part, created? As
though he had heard me ask that question aloud he said
"Nowt n'more t'day. We shears t'morn."

With an impulse to thank her for my whack, I looked
lazily around for Ann. She had gone.

It had been the longest day. It was almost the shortest
night. Our bedroom was full of sunlight and very still in
the heat. Neville, tired out, heaved himself on to the
goosefeather bed and I thought he was already asleep as

I drew just the top sheet over him. The air was still, so hot. Through the open window I heard the churr, churr of a nightjar.

I lay awhile, thinking drowsily of the sheep-shearing next day. Then I remembered and jerked myself awake.

"Neville. Get out of bed." I had to shake him hard.

"No, Ron. No. It can't be tomorrow."

"It isn't. But we've forgotten the most important thing of all."

Still half-asleep and grumbling he knelt beside me.

"Please God, please make Father and Mother better. And bless Edgar and Uncle James and Aunt Jess. And of course Mr. and Mrs. Robinson too I suppose. And Neville and me. And *please* make them better soon. Amen. Into bed now."

When I awoke, I didn't think Ann had let us lie in bed late until I realised she had.

"Get on w' thi breakfas'. Dosta think tha's gotten all day t' do nowt in? Tha's gotten thi weshin' up t' do."

I was drying the last plate when Joe looked in at the scullery door. His milking cap, as white as made no odds, was pulled down so that it pressed on the tops of his ears said "Get a move on, lads. We're ready."

Now Prince was in the shafts, Edgar hoisted Neville into the empty cart and we all piled in after him.

Heat-haze underlined in blue the far side of the Rasser. The sheep-dip was so clear I could count the small brown pebbles lying on the bottom.

Edgar, who came from the sheep country of the Yorkshire wolds, could shear much faster than Joe.

It was Laddie's job now to single out the sheep from the big pen. Then, running and sometimes crouching, he, like a sergeant major, drove them one by one into the narrow double line of hurdles, shepherding them forward for Edgar or Joe to seize.

Neville soon got the hang of being lance-corporal to Laddie. It was my job to pile the fleeces close to the tail of the cart. They were all so much heavier than their snowdrift whiteness looked.

Yesterday I'd been drenched by spray. Now I was soon wiping sweat from my eyebrows.

Freed, the shorn sheep ran joyfully between the second double line of hurdles out into the open Rasser, where the ewes began to graze before lying down in matronly sedateness, and the lambs, shorn last, remembering the carefree frivolity of their babyhood, skipped and gambolled before they too grazed and laid down.

The glorious day wore on. The work was hard but had less of the urgency of dipping day, and only an occasional flurry of excitement when from time to time a light-headed, light-limbed lamb succeeded in leaping a hurdle and the unshorn milled around while Laddie barked commands and I dropped an armful of fleece to help him and lance-corporal Neville restore good order and military discipline.

When the sun had climbed high enough, Edgar knocked off to take the cart to the farm and returned with a second four-gallon cask and more mounds of Ann's sandwiches.

By late afternoon the shearing was done. But not the work. Fists on hips, Joe considered us. He never overworked young animals unnecessarily. He was well content with a highly profitable shearing. I thought he was going to order us to help with loading the ashpoles and hurdles, the wire-netting and the fleeces. Instead, he praised us with laconic unwontedness. "Tha's done weel, lads. Tha can tak' a bit of an easy while Edgar and me clears up."

"There's a fairish sup o' nettle beer left," said Edgar.

Supping, I looked at the results of our labours. I saw, as the sun saw, that the lambs astonished the land as swans astonish the water.

Next morning Ann said "Schooil."

Trudging up Rigton Hill, I noticed an ordinary-looking wild flower. Edgar had told me its name when he'd spotted one in the Home Field. "Yon's Jack-by-the-Hedge. I've see'd it i' Beverley where I comes fro'. Thoo can find Jack-by-t'-Hedge all over England. Nobody ivver takes much notice o' Jack. I'm fond on him. He sticks it through t' hardest winter an' up he comes soon as t' sap rises. Aye, and thoo'll find 'im right through t' summer and on 'e'll run by t' hedge till October happen."

It seemed to me that he'd told me that only yesterday. Yet he'd pointed out the flower way back in March. It made a picture in my mind. And click, another picture took its place.

The year's last fly, crawling on Ann's kitchen wall above the beribboned nail which fastened John Robinson's bicycle brake there.

Why did such pictures appear? Where did they come from and where did they go so quickly? Another picture taking the place of another.

A few weeks later, coming down the hill I heard a voice I knew shouting from the hedge.

CUCKOO. Cuckoo.

I didn't look for him. If I had I might have found that he was Sid Hartley, who loved to torment me. I shouted "CUCKOO to you. In July Sid Hartley must fly. In August, go Sid must."

Sid leaped out at me and we started another fight. I was bigger and stronger now than when I had fought him before. I licked him easily.

Because he wouldn't shake hands afterwards, Alan Church gave him a thumping too.

I took to loitering when school closed. Whatever Iron Ann suspected because of Grandfather Clock's truthful habits, she kept to herself. That note from Dominie Dobson, I reckoned, had settled her.

The June heatwave had long since broken up. September began with sheet lightning followed by sheet rain. Slow Joe was bad-tempered.

Towards the middle of the month the rain cleared away. "Tha's none goin' to schooil till 'arvest's in," said Ann, knowing she had nothing to fear from the Dominie now that every lad able to lend a hand would be absent.

I was tying sheafs of dampish wheat with hairy bands again.

Before the end of November, when the earth spirits had gone back to the earth which bore them, the first blizzard fell upon them to seal them in. "It's ganning t' be a varry 'ard winter," said Edgar. Joe didn't disagree. By Christmas Eve the terrible winter of 1917/18 was upon us.

No question of going back to school in the new, grim year.

No need to see what Candlemas day had to say about the next three months.

The snows of winter had laid siege, not only to Low Moor and its neighbouring farms, but to the whole of Wharfedale, the whole of England. No need for Edgar Artackle to take to his cottage what poacher's windfalls came his way. He was as fast snowed-in at Low Moor as Low Moor itself was snowed in. His day-labourer's wages were merely docked a bit. Every day he and Joe had to tunnel ways through the farmyard to reach the cow-shed, the barn, the pigsty and the stiles.

I followed their tunnellings with a fire-shovel, and bitter as the weather was that kept my young blood warm enough.

Before the real onset the sheep had been driven up from the Rasser and folded close to the farm in the Home Field, soon to be indistinguishable from any field at all.

The pump was a one-armed Snowman with an icicle dripping from his nose. Neville laughed and knocked it off.

What had Ann told me about my hated clogs and leather leggings? I hated them no more. Icicles hung from every snow-masked gutter. It was as well for Low Moor that the men who built it knew winter of old. They had made the roof-trees of farmstead, barn and outbuildings fit to withstand his terrible weight.

Right at the end of February, a quick false thaw came.

One day early in March, I saw far out on the cart track a man struggling to make his way. He made slow progress. I watched him flounder, then struggle on again. Ann came to the kitchen door when I shouted. "Ted," she said, "t' postman." She went indoors again. She reappeared wearing the white apron of respect for visitors. "Mak' thi ways in, Ted. I reckon tha could do wi' a sup o' tea."

"I can that," said the postman.

He handed Ann a letter. She scanned the envelope, her lips moved. She scrutinised the back then pushed the letter into her apron pocket. It was a country habit in days when letters were as infrequent as red letter days to inspect one closely before opening it. To ponder. Who knew what the envelope contained? What tidings of good or ill?

Ted the postman drank his tea and departed, wiping

111

his mouth with the back of his hand.

"Don't stand there gawping," said Ann. "It's time Pharaoh's shed wer cleaned out. If tha can't find owt else t' do after that, Joe will."

A path had been cleared to Pharaoh's shed. I chivvied Pharaoh off his high perch and began to shovel the thick caked droppings. Pharaoh, resenting being driven out, watched me from the top of the snow-covered midden. I stared back at him. For no reason at all I felt a thrill of tension in the pit of my stomach. For no reason at all I screamed at Pharaoh, mocking his own scream. I flung down the shovel.

Suddenly I wanted to do something, anything. I rushed outside. I hurled a snowball at the midden. I would have thrown it at Pharaoh but I still had enough self-control to miss him on purpose.

With a high-pitched squawk he made heavy wing for the snow-weighted roof of the farm.

Neville came out. I fired a snowball at him. It caught him on the ear. Neville yelled "Hi there." I charged the door of Emma's sty and kicked it. Neville came whooping up and he kicked the door. I picked up a broken hedge stake and hammered the stable door. Diamond and Prince made their battering iron shoes shift and stamp.

I ran fast as I could, waving the stake yelling and shouting. Skidding, I fell down in the snow. Neville jumped on my back, rubbed snow down my collar and rolled over and over.

We tumbled and pummelled each other. Gasping, I began to laugh. Neville laughed. I couldn't stop.

I tried to get up, my clog irons slipped and I was flat on my back looking up at the ice-lead sky. I got the feeling that I could do anything, *anything*. There was simply nothing I couldn't do.

Neville said, "Ann's gone to the hen hut. She'll know you're not working. You'll be for it."

I didn't want Neville any more. I got to my feet. "Go inside Nev. Now."

"Why? It's such fun."

I said, "Go. Now." He went.

I clutched handfuls of snow shaping them into hard balls. I piled them at the vantage point. When Ann came out of the hen hut I waited 'till she had taken a few steps then I let fly the first snowball. It hit her in the middle of her back. Before she could turn round I threw another. That struck her shoulder. Ann did not turn round. One after the other I fired the snowballs. Some landed, some missed. The last one hit the kitchen door as she shut it behind her.

With the shutting of the door the feeling of exhilaration left me as suddenly as it had come. Coming to my senses, I was aghast. I knew that had I dared to throw one snowball anywhere near Ann she would have boxed my ears on the instant. She hadn't even turned round.

I wouldn't go in.

Why had that glorious feeling gone?

What had given me the feeling that I could do simply anything at all?

I looked up at the sky again. I could do nothing. I went inside. Ann did not speak. Her mouth was a rat-trap snapped shut.

The oil lamp was already lit. Neville looking as sick-scared as I was feeling, blurted "Ron . . . . "

Ann turned on him.

"Hold thi tongue. It's thi bedtime. Upstairs."

Without daring to look at me he obeyed.

I knew what Ann intended. She'd wait until Joe came in and then I'd get the belting of my life.

"Sit thi down on t'settle," Ann said.

She sat in her own chair opposite me. "Fetch t' Good Book. Tha can read whiles I darns."

The farmhouse kitchen was very quiet. Elbows on the table I read aloud. Silently, Ann darned. So still was the kitchen that even my deaf ear heard Grandfather clock. TICK TOCK TICK TOCK. There was no rap on the table. No warning cough. My gaze was drawn towards Ann's face as though my name had been called. She was looking at me over the tops of her specs. The steel frames were a-glint in the lamplight. The letter lay open on her lap.

I had opened at the story of Jael, the Israelitish woman at the time when the Hebrews were savagely oppressed by their enemy, Sisera. I knew that story well. A phrase in it had caught my fancy when I had chanced on it weeks before. "She put forth butter in a lordly dish." I'd read on to myself as Ann had pondered what significance butter held for her. Now I had chanced again on Jael and Sisera. I read how weary, defeated Sisera had fled out of the lost battle. The stars in their courses had fought against Sisera. In the tent of Jael he had begged her to save his life. The drama gripping me, I read aloud. "Jael stretched forth her hand to the nail and her right hand to the workman's hammer."

As though he knew what was coming, Pharaoh screamed from the darkness.

I stopped reading. TICK TOCK TICK TOCK TICK . . .

Ann said, "Snow'll turn to rain. Thaw'll come in two-three days."

Ann stretched forth her hand to the open letter and her right hand to the workman's hammer. "Ah reckon tha'd best knaw. Thi mother died last September. They buried thi' father six days ago."

114

The nail, so unintentionally driven home, went through the temple of my childish soul. I, the I that was I, who had been born all early in the April ten years before, had been given a name and learned to know that I was Ronald Charles Scriven, the I to whom my father's nod and my mother's shake of the head had meant the whole of what a child can comprehend of God and his own relationship to God, was rent asunder. My heart burst in agony. I saw nothing in the kitchen but the Bible, the book of the God I had been taught to love and trust. To whom I had prayed every night and day, knowing he would make my mother and father well again, asking only that He would make them better soon, soon, soon.

My hands closed the book. And closing it, changed my love and trust into blind hate. The nail, so directly driven by Ann's hammer, had pierced a hole in the shield of the sky, which hides from mortal sight the intolerable light, the burning intensity of the infinite love of God.

Chapter 10

THE DOGE'S PALACE

The first time Uncle James told me the name of my new school was when we were leaving Ellers Road.

"I'm taking you to Crossley's, in Halifax," he said.

I didn't care where it was. All that mattered to me was that I was free for ever from Low Moor Farm and Iron Ann.

In the train from Leeds, I thought about Dominie Dobson. I wondered if my new headmaster would be anything like him. Then it struck me. Unlike North Rigton school, I was going to live in this new one. Would there be more boys at Crossley's? I asked Uncle James.

"Yes, it's of considerable size."

Halifax was all hills. Our tram jerked and lurched and whined up one of the steepest. From the open, toast-racked upper deck I looked out on hump-backed black hills. We passed terraces of black stone houses and, wherever I looked, there rose tall chimneys. They were all pouring out great trailing plumes of black smoke.

"You'll have to apply yourself to your studies, Ronald. With your deafness, you'll find it hard to catch up with your education."

116

"Why, Uncle, Mr. Dobson said I was the brightest boy."

"Mr. Dobson was a good teacher. There is all the difference in the world between a village school and the one you are now going to. Here's where we get off."

We were at the side of a sort of huge park without railings. The grass was rough and a lot greener now we were so high up. There was a large house across this part, which I guessed was my new school.

Though it was just after Whitsuntide, the wind blowing over the hill felt very cold.

Uncle James took a deep breath. "Pure air, Ronald. Straight off the moors."

Instead of making for the big house I was looking at, Uncle James went towards a great iron gate. In the grounds was the biggest building I had ever seen. "Golly," I gasped, "is *that* Crossley's?"

James stopped and looked at it with me. "A splendid edifice," he said.

As we approached it he said, "Don't scuffle your feet, boy."

The Crossley brothers, he told me, owned the biggest carpet factory in the world and had made Halifax famous the world over. They had travelled a lot on business. In Venice one of them had seen the Doge's Palace on the Grand Canal. They wanted to do something for the town which had done so much to make the Crossleys rich. They commissioned an architect to copy the Doge's Palace in local stone and to add a clock tower on top of it.

The building was opened in 1864 as an orphan home and school for four hundred boys and four hundred girls. Uncle James marched me in past big marble busts. "These are the founders," he told me.

He took me into the headmaster's study. G. B. New-

port, M.A., M.Sc. Cantab. He was an Anglo-Indian and
had been amateur wicket keeper for Somerset. I was to
learn later, from the boys of the Lower School, that
they were all perfectly sure he went to bed in his
mortar-board and gown. I didn't know what a mortar-
board was but he wasn't wearing one anyway. A gown?
He was dressed rather like Uncle James but he had put
his arms through a kind of black, short cloak. "Sit
down, Scriven," he said.

He and Uncle James sat in armchairs and I twisted my
toes round the feet of my chair and looked about me as
the headmaster and Uncle James chatted together. Then
James shook hands and went.

Reading the Bible for Iron Ann I knew what the
House of Bondage meant. Low Moor. My uncle
had sold me into a second House of Bondage.
Crossley's.

Crossley's had prefects and sub-prefects. Each new
boy was put under the wing of a fifth-former, his
guardian. Mine was 'Dolly' Speight. He marched me off
to have me outfitted by the matron, Miss Wilkinson —
she was to become one of the most important people in
the whole of my life.

Then he took me along miles of staircases and stone
corridors to the school lavatory. It had been fitted, he
told me, a year or so previously with running hot water
to the fifty-odd washbasins which, at that time, was a
wonder and a marvel.

"Hang your sponge bag and the towel on your own
peg," said Dolly. "Your number is 1644. Now wash."

What I took to be one of the masters came in, he was
in shirt sleeves and began to walk up and down, talking
to Dolly Speight in a language I did not understand. As

he talked, he dropped gouts of lather on the floor in the most lordly fashion. His name was Withrington, he was the school captain and head prefect. He took no notice of me, just another new bug.

The rest of my initiation was spent either in class, in dining hall, on the sports field, fagging for my betters, or hiding in cupboards and ink closets.

Deafness made me an instant butt as it had at North Rigton. In class, from the start to the finish of my formal education, I never heard one word spoken by one teacher. Yet I was put straight into Form III on the strength of Dominie Dobson's support letter.

Crossley's was a marvellous school. Fifty years ahead of its time. Every teacher took pains to coach me. In the last year of the war the staff had to cope, as I had, with adverse odds. Masters were either too old for military service or unfit for it. Their depleted ranks were reinforced by mistresses, mostly unable to discipline boys. They were all dedicated teachers. Possibly because they recognised that I was struggling in the same boat, they gave their own time, freely and warmly, to tutor me.

In my village school, Dominie Dobson had made sure that he got through to me by putting me in a desk at the front of the class. A wily old bird, he used to stand over me, knowing jolly well that the rest could hear him. Those who heard him all right but didn't choose to take in what he said, he dealt with by a method as old-fashioned as himself. A leather strap.

At Crossleys, the size of the class, the size of the room and the echoes from the acoustics made Dominie Dobson's methods as impossible for the teachers as for me. Nevertheless, I responded to each teacher's coaching like an opening flower. I found I had one very strong suit! I was a fluent and voracious reader. I devoured

119

the books they put me on to and ransacked the school library for fodder I found to my taste. I read in the bath, in the loo, on the fire escape. The latter an escape indeed, for because of deafness I was relentlessly tormented in the lower school. I read in the depths of shrubberies. In the gym during playtime, I shinned a pole, swung along a beam to the wall and read there. They chucked rugger boots at me. I read by torchlight in dark in cupboards. I read in class, whether the subject was the one being taught, or not.

So in some subjects I pegged level, in others I lagged behind. In English, history and geography I was well ahead of the pack. In my first end-of-term exam I managed to come third.

Finding at Crossleys that I could, so to speak, hit back, I would have been singularly happy but for one thing. It was a thing which usually befalls those in any way handicapped or different or for whatever reason unlikeable. Bullying.

Bullying was understandable, if not to the bullied. We were all fatherless, motherless, or both. Grief, resentment over dreadful loss, burned inside us all. It gave us impulses to take it out of each other. These feelings were liable to burst out at any time. The hurt hurt one another.

As they were doing far away in the trenches. Three weeks was the average life expectancy of a subaltern in the front line. Casualties in the Navy and the Merchant Navy were as appalling.

In the early days at Crossleys, I had little notion of all this. For me, the enemy sprang out of ambushes. They found me hiding in cupboards and wedged the doors, until I promised to perform ridiculous penances which I knew would make me a laughing stock.

I had the characteristic high-pitched voice of the deaf. They mimicked me. Like a lead pencil screeching on a slate.

It was Ted Williams's form of torment to spring on my back, jam a straw bag over my head and yell "Gallop. Come on old horse, off to the knacker's yard. Gallop."

Wedgwood, the art master, a gentle, elderly soul and one of the great pottery family, put a stop to Ted's harmless fun. Confused, terrorised, I like most of us mistook gentleness for weakness. Wedgey put up with more cheek than any other master would have tolerated. He attended to Ted with a firm hand and a pliant cane.

So, like other small fry struggling in the shallow rapids of the lower school, I had to swim or sink. I swam, against the stream. Set upon myself, I envied the mischief others got up to.

Like every big clock in the land, the one in Crossleys' tower had been silent for years. Caliban Clough could climb and he did. Out of the dorm window he went, along a stone ledge, then up, using the crevices of the Doge's noble facade for finger and toe holds. He climbed into the clock tower and was in bed again pretending to be asleep when the clock boomed out over Halifax, striking midnight and wild joy as the town started awake, convinced that the strokes signalled victory and the end of the war.

The armistice, a week later, let loose on the school the pealing tongues of bells, and hundreds of tins of Mackintosh's toffee.

We erupted from our classrooms.

Excitement swept us through corridors, up staircases, through dorms, down again and into the sacred studies of sixth-form prefects. Mortar-boarded, but unbelievably without his gown, the headmaster was cheered by us all every time he was seen.

In the wake of grace after food we were too excited to eat, the bugles of the school's troop of scouts sounded The Last Post. We surged into the gym to get up a concert. Tables were dragged down the corridor from the dining hall to make a stage. Dolly Speight inked a moustache on. He turned his collar back to front and started off the show with a sing-song. Tipperary.

We all sang at the tops of our voices, all the war songs we knew. Pack Up Your Troubles. Goodbye. Keep the Home Fires Burning. Then there was a hilarious hotch-potch of card-tricks, a makeshift magician — in real life Hanson, the French master — called one of the boys, Gilbert Backhouse, on to the stage. He placed a screen in front of Gilbert, who slipped down a gap between two of the tables. Hanson knocked the screen flat and pointed with his wand to the back of the gym. "Abra-cadabra." And there was Gilbert. But it wasn't him. It was his identical twin brother Clifford. In the mood we were in it brought the house down.

I was sharing the top of a radiator with my friend, Beaky Umpleby. He nudged me off it. I didn't mind Beaky using my new school nickname. "Go on, Crippen. Give 'm Kipling's IF." I gulped my way up on to the stage. If it had been the Rasser it couldn't have seemed larger. I opened my mouth. I don't remember how I got through the lines but I did remember the words for I had them by heart. "If you can fill the unforgiving minute with sixty seconds worth of distance run," I finished with a rush, "Yours is the earth and everything that's in it, and which is more you'll be a man, my son."

Instead of the howls of derision I'd expected, everyone cheered and stamped until my knees felt trembly and I was all choked up.

Wild rumours ran through the school that Old Harrison,

122

the geography master, had been seen waltzing in the masters' Common Room with Miss Macaulay, the history mistress.

Caliban Clough had gone crackers, raided the school rifle range in the basement and shot Miss Wilkinson. Where? Where all boys everywhere would have said Miss Wilkinson had been shot.

In the deepening dusk out into the grounds we ran, we saw all over Halifax signal rockets soaring at random. The bells of St. Jude's and every other church had gone bats in their belfries. Even I could hear the clamour. And suddenly on Beacon Hill, we all yelled as we saw the wind-tossed flames, flaring to heaven.

We were all rushed to the dining hall for a late, disorganised supper.

It took a week for our feverish excitement to cool down. Then the end-of-term exams were upon us.

Everything seemed very flat as we tried to settle badly to our studies. Cocky little Hanson, who refereed house rugger matches, had somehow contrived to give me a smattering of elementary French. This, like Latin, was a barbed wire entanglement of a language through which I had to scramble as best I could. It was difficult enough for me to get the correct pronunciation of new words in my mothertongue, without having to get the hang of French which the native-born don't speak as it is spelled. I was last but one in French, and last in Latin.

The headmaster took me in Latin, elementary chemistry and scripture. Scripture was an unintentional legacy from Iron Ann. I drove through that paper as furiously as I could and came in second.

Miss Macaulay had piloted me through the English Channel and beyond it through the historic Straits of Dover. If you love English you can't but love the mother of the language, history, she told me.

In the exams I finished third in a field of thirty-two.

My success stupefied me. As soon as the form result was known, Beaky claimed some of the credit. "If Crippen had listened to me," he told anyone who'd listen to him, "he'd have done a lot better in French and stinks."

When the first of the results had been pinned on the notice board, the mood of the school changed. Elated, we banged desk lids to the ritual chant of 'No more Latin, no more French, no more sitting on a hard, cold bench.' We were breaking up. Those who were leaving queued outside the head's study to be handed their leavers' bibles.

Miss Wilkinson supervised the packing of suitcases, deputised reliable slave drivers to ensure that everyone caught the right train from the right platform.

Miss Wilkinson knew boys inside-out and to bounce. We milled round her. She knew how we all hated the school uniform, the ugly grey capes in particular.

"Go on, Crippen," shouted Beaky. "Tell Miss Wilkinson she can bury the lot."

"Go on yourself. You tell her."

Wonderful, wonderful. We wouldn't have to wear them in the hols.

Halifax was a stronghold of nonconformity. Church of England boys – and I was one – on Sundays were marched in crocodiles to the nearest C of E church, St. Jude's. Matron knew that each boy in the crocodile felt that his uniform shouted 'orphan,' setting him apart.

We all saw families going to church together. Children holding their parents' hands. We all felt that it was a shameful thing to be an orphan. I did. And I knew by their faces my schoolfellows felt the same. We never spoke about it.

I could see now what I could not see all those years ago. Crossleys was a very well-endowed charity. Some of the boys and girls were both fatherless and motherless. Most belonged to one-parent families. In the last year of the first war that meant that a Crossley child was fatherless. A widowed mother had a bitter struggle to exist. Crossleys lightened that burden by feeding, clothing and educating those children.

Crossleys also admitted children who were orphans in the full sense, as I was, but whose people were able to pay.

Miss Wilkinson knew who the few were who were paid for. So did the headmaster and the headmistress. Nobody else knew. I did not know until much later on during my years at the school that Uncle James paid my fees, not out of his own pocket, though I believe he would have done had it been necessary, but from my patrimony.

People like Miss Wilkinson did not regard the care of the orphans as an act of Christian charity. To her, it was a natural thing, just part of what it meant to be a Christian. She knew well enough how many paid lip-service to religion. Her Christianity encompassed those also.

A first-class organizer, Miss Wilkinson saw to it that all of us were ticketed, docketed and our homeward routes worked out to the last detail.

Masters, mistresses or prefects marched us down to the station in batches, nearly all of us at the end of a long term empty-pocketted.

In the New Year of 1919 I re-entered the Doge's Palace with my brother Neville in tow. He was bursting with joy. I felt very much the older brother with a duty to fight his battles for him.

Before the term was a month old he was fighting my battles for me.

Chapter 11

MISS WILKINSON

"Mouldy old Halifax," said Neville cheerfully as we got out of the train.

The winter term of 1922 held no problems for him. At eleven-minus he was vigorously a-swim in the third form. I'd be fifteen in April and I knew I must do some hard spadework, for the School Certificate was rather more than a year away and I knew my weaknesses now.

I said "You bung off on the tram, Nev. You can take my suitcase too. I'll walk up. I've a lot to think about."

"Right-ho," said Neville. "Bet you're fed up with all that swotting in the hols."

The January clouds were low, like my spirits. I was going back under a cloud.

By my own standards I'd done badly in the end of term exams. That wasn't the worst of it by a long chalk. I'd fallen foul of my headmaster.

Newport took me in chemistry, my worst subject. The text book in stinks was *Elementary Chemistry* by G. B. Newport, M.A., M.Sc. My own copy was more than a bit battered and its red cover had come loose. An old dodge occurred to me. From the time when I'd hidden *Comic Cuts* in the cover of *Robinson Crusoe*. Last term I'd slipped the chemistry text inside my desk and replaced it with something nearer to my fancy.

The shadow of my headmaster had fallen over the pages just too late to warn me. Newport had locked up the book. "H'mm. *Clubfoot the Avenger*. By Valentine Williams. Was it your English master who recommended this classic as required reading? I'll see you after prep, Scriven."

He'd given me three stingers on each palm for that. I knew I'd earned them. What really hurt had been his sarcasm at the expense of my beloved Robb. I thought Newport had a down on him. And Robb was a sick man. He was sometimes absent for three or four days at a time.

The nearer I got to school, the more I was convinced that I hadn't been moved up into the fifth. And bang, I told myself, had gone my chance of being made a sub-prefect, slim chance anyway because of my deafness.

The CLANG of the iron gate at the side entrance said as much to me.

My friends were waiting for me beside the green baize notice board. Bill Fox, Hugh Miles, Shiny Wright. Friends I'd won the hard way, the way which binds friendship fast. Neville was hovering behind them. He whooped "Ron, Ron. The head's made you a sub-prefect. You're in the lower fifth."

I said, "I've had my leg pulled before."

"It's true, old son," said Bill Fox.

"Newport has three Gods," said Miles. "God, Kipling and cricket. Especially Kipling.

"He likes to think of himself as a beast but a just beast," said Shiny Wright.

"There it is, on the board. See for yourself."

"Hooray," shouted Neville. "Now you're a sub-prefect I can do as I like. Go on pantry raids with Pip Musther. Have pillow fights after lights out."

"If I catch you," I said "You'll get six of the best." I felt cock-a-whoop. I chased Neville up the corridor.

My world had turned right side up, and the jolt that gave me altered my relationship with Neville. So far, in school, we'd lived in different worlds. He had his own interests, his own friends, his own hobbies. I had mine. We belonged to separate houses.

"Newport's idea," Fox had said, "Is to keep us on our toes. Hence house matches, cups and shields and all that – modelled on the Public Schools."

By dividing the school into four houses of Trojans, Spartans, Vikings and Paladins, Newport had deliberately turned the old Roman motto, Divide and Conquer, inside out.

Keen rivalry in house matches ensured the strength of a school team which would stand united when it took on other schools.

The head's policy of placing brothers in different houses paid off well. Given authority, this boy would use it to favour a younger brother. That boy would lean the other way and publicly demonstrate his impartiality by being too hard on a younger brother. So, in theory, the whole school was nicely balanced.

I felt, without being able to analyse, the stresses and strains of human loyalties. I was too damn hard on young Neville. If he'd been in my house, a Trojan, he'd have caught it worse. Because he was a Spartan, he was less immediately under my eye. Neville, younger, knew even less of these complications. With ferocious loyalty, he had fought any lesser of his own fry who had dared in his hearing to jeer at my deafness. Now Neville was positive that as I was a sub-prefect, I could show my brotherly loyalty to him. My loyalty to Robb was so wholehearted that it led me into making misjudgements about the way Newport, as I thought, treated him unfairly.

The complexity of this close-meshed network of human relationships I partly felt, partly guessed at the time and did not begin to understand until years later. What I did understand right away was that as a sub-prefect I didn't have to ask the head's permission to go into the town in my free time.

With Bill Fox, like me rejoicing in a new freedom, I hared off to Skircoat Green Library. A brisk trot on a winter day made the friendly little library all the cosier. We went back each with an armful of books.

Going into school I ran into Robb. He said, "Ah, Scriven. I want a word with you. Come along to the masters' Common Room."

What was up? What had I done or not done? It was Robb's custom to set essays and quite often not mark them until two or three weeks later.

Robb said, "Let's have a look at this lot. Take a pew, Scriven. Ha. *A Dream in the Luxembourg*. Didn't know you'd come across Aldington."

"I think he's marvellous, sir. I . . . I am *in* those gardens with him. I mean, I've only dipped into it."

"He's a good poet. And what's this? Buchan's *Thirty-nine Steps*? Not . . . " he chuckled "*Clubfoot the Avenger*?"

So he'd heard about that, another chance for Newport to get at him. Sitting down, he felt for his pipe.

"The more omnivorously you read while your eyes are young, the better. Penny dreadfuls like *King Richard the Second*. Shilling shockers like *Macbeth*. If you're

129

going to make a poet — and I think you might be — Scriven, I suggest an exception to the general rule. Don't read your contemporaries until you are forty. Poets are born, like everyone else. The old name for a poet was a 'maker'. If you're going to be one, you must make what you can of this world of ours. The less you are influenced by your contemporaries, the better. Read, read, read all other poets. Back to Anon who, and not Chaucer, was the father of English poetry."

"Betuene Mershe and April," I said "When spray beginneth to spring . . . "

"That's Anon," said Robb and added, half to himself "An hendy hap ichab Ghent, ichot it is from heaven me sent my love from woman kind is lent and lit on Alisoun." Robb gave me one of his rare smiles. "Anon's poetry flows from the rills and springs of the high hills. The lark taught him to sing Lauds, and the blackbird to sing Evensong. Chaucer is a fountain, yes. A fountain fed from all the springs and rills. The source of the great river of English poetry." Robb had let his pipe go out. He drew on it and said, "My tobacco jar is at your elbow. Shove it across, there's a good chap."

Robb's tobacco jar was topped, not by a lid but a small green book.

"Palgrave's *Golden Treasury*."

I watched Robb tamp down the tobacco in his pipe. I could have listened to Robb for hours. This was great stuff. But Robb said, "I've pi-jawed enough." He opened the book and wrote on the fly-leaf. Then he pushed the green book across. He had written, "Drink deep, or taste not the Pireian spring." I'd watched him as he signed it.

Robb's skin was slightly yellowish. It was stretched tightly across his broad forehead. He was sweating a little at the roots of his hair. I saw pain in his eyes. Robb had been shell-shocked and gassed in France. That was why he was absent for a few days now and then. He had a generous, full quirky mouth and loved to banter Newport about Kipling.

My brash belief that Newport had a down on him could not have been farther from the truth. The head knew that Robb, a Manchester Grammar School man, was an inspired teacher of English. One of those choice spirits of whom Kipling himself had said, "For their work continueth, broad and deep continueth far beyond their knowing."

Refreshed beyond my knowing by Robb's talks with me, I plunged into the term's work as joyously as after a house match and a hot bath I dived into the school swimming bath.

And I duly thumped Neville when I caught him raiding the pantry with Pip Musther.

I had two ambitions now. To cram into my head as much poetry as I could and to get my School Certificate next year.

Towards the end of March, I turned out for a house match, Trojans v Spartans.

Broomfield, the school sports ground, was a mile away from Skircoat Road. Both teams, in shorts and the house shirts only, mingled together as we streamed downhill.

Cocky Hanson, a neutral housemaster, was to referee. We were warm enough, in spite of a sleety wind, when Hanson blew his whistle for the kick off.

It was a ding-dong affair. No score at half-time.

Lemons were rushed to us by our supporters. I bit into mine, rind and all, and it spurted down my throat gloriously.

Rugger to me was a joy and an exasperation. A front

row forward, I heaved and shoved with the best of them in the scrums. In open play I heard Hanson tootling and hooting on his whistle if I happened to be near him. Mostly I wasn't and followed the course of the game by sight.

The ground was a porridge of grass, mud and sleet. I had to play as me, an individual. I seldom heard the yell of "Pass" when I had the ball. Nearly time, and still no score. I longed to make up for being a poor team-player by touching down between the posts with a winning try just before the whistle blew.

Then I heard Hanson tootling and a second later got the smack of a greasy Rugger ball straight in my face. As the ball bounced, I caught it more by luck than anything. My moment of glory was upon me. I tucked the pill under my arm and ran. I could dodge and swerve — TOOTLE — I crossed the enemy's 25 line. There was only their full-back between me and the goal posts. A scurry of sleet only made my blood hotter. I swerved round the full-back throwing himself forward to tackle me. In a burst of all-out physical endeavour I went over the line and touched down, flat on my face.

Glory, glory, glory. I'd done it. As I got to my feet I could hear them cheering. I shook my head. Glory, the Spartans were waving and cheering as loudly as my own Trojans.

Out of the hullaballoo, close up I heard one voice I knew, "Scriven, you ass. Didn't you hear the Ref whistling for a forward pass when I slung the ball at you?"

It was Bill Fox. And he was laughing. Everybody was laughing. The Spartan cheers had been cheers of irony. I'd made a complete howling fool of myself. And this time I did hear Hanson.

"Time. No score. Re-play next Wednesday."

Like a pack of foxhounds, liver and tan, lemon and mud the two teams went streaming off the field, their supporters like foot-followers whooping in the rear.

Overhauling me, Bill clapped a hand on my shoulder. "Hard luck, old son. Cheer up. You did have a damn good go."

Humiliated to the marrow, I shrugged his hand away.

When the teams got back, the story of Scriven's latest piece of tomfoolery would spread all over Crossleys.

Dejectedly, I lagged farther and farther behind. Soon I dropped to a walk. I just didn't want to face them. They'd all gone in long before I slouched towards the side gate. Beside it was a public seat. A fat man, raggedly shabby was standing on it. A Weary Willie of a fellow except that he was waving his arms about and orating. His audience was a nursemaid with a pram. And two of the greyly unemployed leaning against the wall. The orator was easy to hear, so I listened.

"I was a sinner of the blackest dye." He rolled the whites of his eyes. "But I'm not now. I was saved from the pit by a Salvation Army lassie, God bless her, she came into the Cock and Bottle with a *War Cry*. She told me 'Sinner, repent. Be washed in the blood of the lamb.'"

I huddled my shoulders. Both teams would have been bathed and changed by now.

"Aye," groaned the ex-sinner, "She took me into t' town hall square. She guided me 'and while I signed t' pledge on t' big drum."

"Oh aye?" said one of the unemployed. "Then what was tha doin' reeling out o' t' White Bear at closing time?"

The sleet changed suddenly to snow and his audience vanished. My teeth chattered as I cut through the gym to the baths. Everyone had gone.

Soaking in the hot water I wondered why my teeth

were still chattering. I dressed. Whatever time was it?

I met some of them leaving the dining hall for prep. I didn't care that I'd missed tea. I hurried into prep.

In the morning I felt lousy. I swallowed some breakfast. My form-room turned itself round. I retched.

"What's the matter, Scriven?" Someone put an iceberg hand on my forehead.

"Knowles, take him straight to matron."

Matron was in her office. As Knowles, his hand on my elbow, guided me in I caught sight of myself in a mirror. My eyes nearly startled themselves out of my head. They were wide awake open and they sparkled brilliantly.

Miss Wilkinson didn't feel my forehead. She said "Knowles, find Nurse Black and ask her to come to the sick bay."

The whiteness of the sick bay, ceiling, walls, beds seemed to me to swim together dizzily. My stomach heaved and everything in it, which I'd been fighting to keep down, came up. The stuff clammily spewed out of my mouth, down my nostrils, and it hurt.

I'd tried to lurch away from Miss Wilkinson's hand when the slosh came, to spew on the floor. Instead, I was sick all over the counterpane. Realising what I'd done, I felt a second spasm of shame.

Her voice, matter of fact, "Get some more up if you can. Go on. Try. No? Let's get you out of your clothes, then. I'm going to put you in bed."

She put me between sheets of ice and fire. No matter how I tried to clamp them together my teeth chattered. All I longed for was warmth and sleep.

"Hold on," I said to myself. Hold on to what? I coughed — and that cough gave me the answer. Not to cough again.

To cough was pain. To cough was torture. Not to cough was to be tortured on the rack.

Time ceases to exist for the tortured. There is only the here, the now of pain.

Miss Wilkinson said "Spit in this cup." The stuff I spat was rusty and every time I spat a tearing, searing pain wrenched at my chest.

"Spit." Miss Wilkinson's sleeve was blue. Miss Wilkinson's sleeve wasn't blue, but white. It wasn't Miss Wilkinson. It was Nurse Black. The racking, rasping pain became worse.

And now Miss Wilkinson was back. Her hand in her blue sleeve was helping the torturers. Helping them to tighten the dreadful vice which was cracking my ribs every time I tried to draw breath, Miss Wilkinson urged the torturers to tighten the vice harder, harder.

Miss Wilkinson was a fiend, not a woman. Why hadn't I known that when I thought she was a woman? A good woman. Kind to me. Kind to everyone. I got the answer. Fiends disguise themselves. Miss Wilkinson disguised herself as Nurse Black. She could afford to do, now that she had me at her mercy. She was cunning. She disguised herself as Gran. Gran was saying, "Oh Ronald, my poor lamb, my poor lamb."

Suddenly, she disguised herself as Neville. There he was sitting beside my bed saying, "Hello, Ron." Then I knew it really was Neville.

I said, "Quick, get me a drink of water. Miss Wilkinson won't give me any, I'm dying for a drink."

"I can't, Ron," said Neville. "Miss Wilkinson has only allowed me to come and see you for a minute or two. Ron, Ron. You're awfully ill. The whole school prayed for you at assembly, Ron."

I said "Fill a hot water bottle with cold water. Hide it

under your waistcoat. Quick, do what I say."

Neville wasn't there any more. Then he was. He said, "Here you are, Ron. Slip it under the sheets."

Secretly I unscrewed the stopper and drank and drank. The crisis came that night.

Each breath I tried to draw stabbed and seared me. Somebody's hand, it seemed to me, was trying to slacken the vice which was crushing my chest.

I turned my face to the wall. There was a hairline crack in the white paint. Out of that crack I saw a white slug oozeing. I knew it was coming to kill pain.

Who was pulling at my shoulder to tug me away from the white slug? My blurred sight cleared. An arm in a blue sleeve came between me and the slug.

Miss Wilkinson said, "Ronald, you are very ill. You are not going to die. I will not let you die."

I fought against her hand, her voice. I was too weak to resist. Miss Wilkinson pulled me away from the wall.

Everything which was left of the I which was me gave itself into her hands.

The hands of Miss Wilkinson were the hands of mercy, the hands of healing. Throughout my delirium she had been with me. In the brief, lucid interval as she turned my face from the wall I heard her voice. "As Jacob wrestled all night with an angel, Lord, help me to wrestle with the angel of death. There."

All night her hands sponged my body, wiping away the fever sweat. From head to foot she sponged, sponged and sponged my body. My mind was God knows where.

In the small, grey hours when life is at its lowest ebb the souls of the dying drift out to sea. I drifted on that tide. It washed me ashore many hours later, alive.

I opened my eyes from sleep. I knew who I was, and where I was. The curtains had been drawn wide apart.

They were fluttering. Birds, alive, alive, were dipping and swooping past the open window. I loved them because they were there. Because I was seeing them.

I felt weaker than a kitten. Then I saw Miss Wilkinson. She was lying on a bed next to mine. She looked unutterably weary, but her face was turned towards me and she was smiling.

"I'm hungry," I said.

"Splendid," said Miss Wilkinson. "It has been many days since you've had a meal. What would you like?"

"I could eat a whale."

"A piece of plaice, I think, will meet the occasion."

When the tray was brought in she had added a tiny glass of flowers.

During my slow convalescence, she told me that Gran *had* been to see me but that I had not known her though she had stayed a whole afternoon with me.

James, she said had looked in but, she smiled, I had been talking twenty to the dozen to Nurse Black who wasn't there. A little like James himself, she added "He was most concerned about you." I couldn't believe it. Not *know* Gran. Not *see* Uncle James.

Time has not sponged away my memory of the house match and my ignominious part in it. Time has not sponged away my memory of the sinner of the blackest dye rescued by a *War Cry* and a Salvation Army lassie.

My memory of the delirium of pneumonia and pleurisy in the sick bay has been all but wiped out.

When time stops, I will forget Miss Wilkinson. I didn't understand her. Which of us, at Crossleys did? Or could? Bill Fox, who used to play chess with her now and then? Miss Wilkinson, who mothered generation after generation of the motherless and if she had favourites never let them know it.

What kept her going? I can only hazard a guess. Love
. . . and the knowledge that the world, glory be, has
never been short of Miss Wilkinsons. But the woman
herself? What was she really like, in flesh and blood?
What thoughts, what dreams, what emotions made her
what she was? I, who owe my life to her, do not know.
But God, who made her, does.

Chapter 12

SUMMER WITH FLOWERS THAT FELL

For ten days I was unsettled, like the weather. Like the glass I was physically up a bit and down a bit. When I could I went out with my Uncle on his surgery rounds. More often, Neville went too. On the last day before he went back to school we sat together in the back seat not talking much. For the first time in my life, Neville seemed to me stronger than I.

"Wish I were going back with you, Nev."

"You must be cuckoo. Wish I could stay on in Milford."

That evening Uncle Harold said, "Better come along to the surgery, Admiral."

I lay down on the black, horsehair couch he had inherited from his father. It prickled the back of my neck. "Open your shirt. H'mmmm."

With his stethoscope he sounded my chest back, front and sides. He pushed a thermometer under my tongue and kept it there while he put his fingers over the pulse of my wrist.

"I thought as much," he said.

He shook down the thermometer. "South Milford

isn't doing you as much good as I hoped it would. You need somewhere more bracing. Your Aunt Ciss and I have been concerned about you and have decided to send you to Masham, the market town of Wensleydale. You'll stay a few weeks with a relative of ours, Mrs. Ryder, she was a Scriven before she married. She has a son, older than you, called Ted. Tom will run you over tomorrow."

Somewhere new. Another place to be sent to. Oh well.

"May I borrow a book or two to take with me?"

"I've got the *Golden Treasury*. You may like to take that with you. Some Wordsworth and Mr. Sponges *Sporting Tour*. Some first-class invective in that. Bring them back."

We went by way of Harrogate. I began to talk. Tom's answers were laconic.

"Uncle Harold says the Corporation ran the gas mains under the magnesium springs in the Valley Gardens and perforated them so that the gas made all the waters taste nearly as nasty as the sulphur water."

"Aye, Master Ronald. The nastier they tasted, the more good folk believed the stuff was doing 'em."

The Bean climbed and climbed. In mid-afternoon we crested a steeper hill.

Tom braked. "Masham."

It was like looking down into a deep cup with a piece bitten out of the far rim. At the bottom of the cup was a hump-backed bridge over a winding river. In the water meadow at our side of the bridge a cricket match was being played.

Whenever one sees a village match, either the bowler is walking away from the wicket or the field is being re-set for changing overs. Never does one see a ball bowled or a batsman strike one nor a fielder make a catch.

"I'd like to play cricket again, Tom. I scored three, not out, for South Milford last summer."

"Second eleven. Happen Masham team'll let you have a game or two. Think on what Doctor said and don't overdo it now."

At the gate of a small garden full of soft-fruit bushes, a small, dark, vivid lady was waiting. She ran out to the car.

"There you are, Ronald. You won't remember me but I knew you when you were in your nappies. Ted's working but he'll be back at teatime. Come in. You'll stop for tea, Tom?"

"No thankee, ma'am. I've got to get back for the first surgery."

He flipped the peak of his chauffeur's hat, and drove off.

Apple pie. Thick yellow cream. A wodge of pale Wensleydale cheese. I was having a second go when Ted came home.

In the new world, mine, like Bevis's New Formosa, for the exploring, all things were bright and beautiful. And poetry was in all that I looked at.

The river drew me as it drew the swallows and the dragonflies. In their candelabra, green, green by the waterside, the chestnuts' lovely candles were lighted, as it seemed to me, by the young May moon, so bravely did they blaze when daylight came.

One Saturday evening at deepening dusk Ted said, "Come on, Ron. I'll show you how to walk by night."

"Ted. You're not to take him poaching."

"Of course not, Mother."

141

Dew like recent rain on the grass drenched my bare soles as we crossed the water meadow, our shoes slung round our necks. High over the wood at the farther side of the river the last dragon's blood-dregs of sunset were draining from the sky. It was the dark of the once young moon.

"We can cross here," said Ted. "Give me your hand. Don't slip."

The rippling water pushed against my legs above the knee. The small fry tickled and nibbled me.

We waded ashore and I wondered if Ted could see like an owl, he was so sure of his way.

"Stop." He spoke very close to my good ear. A match spurted, the sudden flame dazzling me. It vanished as suddenly. But a glow began to spread.

"I made this dark lantern from two empty cocoa tins and a bull's eye."

He shaded with one palm the narrow pencil of light which drew the bole of a tree, then Ted's palm rubbed it out with darkness and the pencil sketched again.

His free hand gripped my shoulder. The pencil of light lighted a woodland path sloping to the river behind us. Along this path with the lurching gait of a drunken sailor a badger in a pepper-and-salt coat nosed forward. Not until his nose butted into the spread of my naked toes did he take alarm. Then, cursing like a hazing mate, he lurched off into the wood.

"You can hand over that poacher's lantern," said a deep voice. "Now turn out your pockets."

The keeper had come upon us so quietly that not even Ted's alert ears had warned him.

"I'm not poaching," he said. "I'm just showing our visitor what the woods are like at night."

"You can tell that to the Masham bench on Monday

morning, my young cock sparrow. Turn out those pockets I say."

Ted produced a hanky, reasonably white in the beam the keeper turned on it from Ted's own lantern. A jack knife. A shilling and two ha'pence. Five Woodbines and a box of matches.

"That's the lot."

"And this chap? Name of Ronald, isn't he? Staying with your mother."

"Yes. He's green."

"What do you think I am? As green as a white cabbage? But for your mother and the respect I had for your dad, I'd turn you over. Now get the hell out of here."

Once our bare feet were on the cobblestones of the main street Ted began to laugh.

"If you hadn't been with me, I bet the old devil would have made me turn my jack sleeves inside out. I've three night lines hooked to the lining of one and half a dozen wire snares up the other."

They'd picked sides for cricket.

"Where's Harry?"

"He's not turned up."

"Can I play, please? I played for South Milford."

"South Milford? Where the hell's South Milford? Bugger off."

I began to pick up. I felt stronger. By Whitsun, the chestnut candles had almost burned their sockets and Neville joined me. I took him joyously downstream to a wooden bridge built for practice by the sappers in the unforgotten war. It was a temptation to any boy in his wrong mind. We lay out on one of their beams in midstream and caught minnows in a jam jar on a length of string. As we took turns to haul up the jar, the drops of water trickling down the string winked in the sunlight like the eyes of the minnows.

"Look, dogs. Lots of them," said Neville suddenly. He looked downstream.

A pack of liver-and-tan otter hounds, their sterns feathering like the blades of oars, their noses to the creeping-buttercupped, moon-daisied grass were working their way up on either bank. Half a dozen men with long poles and a rabble of boys yelled on the Bassett hounds. Men, boys and hounds were as often splashing through the water as they were trampling the grass. Men and boys crossed and recrossed the shallows where the Yore ran close and deep on the south bank or the north.

We were wildly excited.

"Hi, you two." Ted, close on the heels of the huntsmen, pointed to the north, the nearer bank. Half the hunt had passed before we swung our way from beam to beam to join him.

"Run."

We tried to keep up with him. "Wait for me."

Ted knew every twist and turn of his native river, so close to home. The sun-glints, the mirrored willows where the water ran slow and deep, the boulder-broken shallows, like miniature rapids, where Yore ran on a loose rein made my heart pound with joy.

I only noticed how my lungs were straining when Neville drew level with me and I remembered Uncle Harold's warning.

Ted slowed, but not because of either of us. He was listening hard.

"She's making for the watermill. Come on." He altered course, came on a woodland ride and went faster. I hung on.

All the jays in the wood were telling tales as though betraying a fox in covert, not an otter in the river. They shouted so loudly that I heard them.

The three of us came out almost in the shadow of the water mill below the spire-pointing finger of Masham Church.

Ted flung himself headlong on the grass and so did I.

The mirroring water reflected the dazzle of the blue of the sky that was the surface, the skin of the river. The light changed, the reflection shifted.

"There."

I saw, in the river, a thing of beauty and wonder. An otter, her body sleek in a chain-mail of silver bubbles and swimming for her life.

As swiftly as I saw her, she was gone.

"She's slipped them," said Ted. "She's gone into her bolt-hole under the roots of that alder."

Wide were the water meadows, wide where Fir Wood leaned to the waterside. Swans, plumaged in summer with winter snow, floated, imaged on the current's flow.

St. Bartholomew's day, the 24th August was a day of days for Masham.

Ted had told me all about it for days beforehand. I, the stranger, knew that the fair was not for me. But it might be fun.

"I'm off with my mates," he said when the great day came.

St. Bartholomew. The very name had the ringing ding of a blacksmith's hammer on the anvil. I watched the Romany caravans roll into the market square. The bump of their wheels on the cobblestones set pots and pans and kettles jangling against the sides of the wagons. Their arrival was a burst of colour, a swirl of movement, a steam-organ blare of sound.

145

Up went the huge swings. Hoop-la's, coconut shies, rifle ranges were conjured out of the cobblestones. And into this whirl of excitement which made my eyes dance came the lads hell-bent for the fair.

Farm lads from villages up and down the dale, lads scrubbed and tubbed, tanned faces a-shine hot-footed it, hot-collared in their Sunday-best navy blue. Work freed, farm-free, the fair was all for them.

Each fresh drove swelled the crowd. They jostled and bustled around me and I knew none of them. I felt their excitement. They shouted greetings to those they knew. Their pockets jangled with coins saved up since Easter-tide. And I was in it. The noise added to the excitement and the excitement added to the noise.

Lonelier and more sorry for myself than ever, I mooched around. I looked at the bearded lady who looked like a strong man. I eyed the strong man, who looked like a bearded lady.

The fair was a nosegay of a thousand smells. Naphtha fumes and candyfloss. Hot pies and peas and the nutty smell of shag tobacco. Beer and brandysnap. The reeking engine oil and the river mist.

All these smells blended and yet were different, as I went from stall to stall, from rifle range to the great mechanical roundabout.

Gilded cocks and snow-white hens alongside red nostril-flaring horses sliding down and up, each on their own brass-gold, barley-sugar-sticked twisted poles.

The lonelier I felt in that fairground, the more I wanted to join in.

The blare and glare was having its effect on those who *were* the crowd. I sensed, without understanding what I sensed, that the crowd was changing. The approach of dusk was dissolving that crowd into groups, into coteries.

Groups of boys stood close to the big swings. Drifting, I joined them.

There was movement all about. Swings up a-flying, down a-sweeping.

Girls a-standing in the swing-bars, hair-a-streaming, skirts a-flying, up and high, swoosh and down and up and up, with girls a-screaming to go over the bar, and screeching not to.

Girls a-giddy from the roundabouts a-stumbling, accidentally on purpose into the arms of boys accidentally on purpose standing ready to catch them.

I lingered, then wrenched myself away. I had no girl who wanted me to catch her.

Girls, shy-saucy, cheeking the boys. Boys, scoffing, deriding, showing off boys.

Girls' eyes. Boys' eyes. A-scanning, a-searching each other's.

Yearning for that one spark in a glance that would fire the purpose of all their play: the kiss-chase.

In the light-shot shadows between the naphtha flares and the roundabout, I felt a tickle at the back of my neck. I whipped round.

She was smiling at me in all the loveliness of herself. The one girl at the fair, the one girl in all the world for me. She turned and ran. As she ran, a naphtha flame struck fire-glints from her chestnut hair.

Loneliness, uncertainty, hesitation, the fear of being rebuffed went in that one fire-glint. I'd envied the other boys, knowing what they were after. This girl had challenged me to be myself. Challenged me to run after her.

In a pool of shadows, behind the roundabout I caught her.

"Let me go. Let me go."

"I won't, 'till you've paid me a forfeit."

"I won't. Let me go."

She fought me to twist her wrist out of my grasp.

"All right. What's the forfeit?"

"Tell me your name."

"I won't pay unless you tell me your name first."

"I bet you know it already. It's Ronald."

She threw back her head and laughed.

"In Masham? Of course I know."

"You cheat. I'm the one who calls the forfeit. I asked your name first."

"I'll tell when I choose."

With a snatch as swift as it was unexpected she slipped my grasp and ran out of the square.

In the deepening darkness of Masham Lane I caught her. She paid her forfeit.

Stars like a hive of silver bees let loose gathered honey from the field of heaven.

Sweeter, ah, sweeter was the honey of her lips. She sealed her forfeit with a kiss.

Softened by distance, the lights of the fair on the hill behind us, reflected from the sky, made pools of shadow under the hedges inky.

Soft and distant too, the music blended with the excitement in my blood.

Her heart beat against mine.

"Rose, Rose, my Rose of Wensleydale." That was the last I remember of Masham fair. Oh, Rose, my rose of all roses, my first love, my lost love.

Chapter 13

FARE WELL

I spent the last week of the Easter hols of 1923 with Hugh Miles. I didn't sleep much for three nights. Hugh lived right on a main traffic road leading out of Huddersfield.

Like my Uncle James, he was a great walker. He walked me up into the hills. The name of Huddersfield arrives from 'Odin's Field' and the hill streams flashed and gashed the ghylls and ravines in the strengthening sun. Deep in those Yorkshire moors was some of the roughest going in England.

Unable to keep up with Hugh, I called "Hi. Slow down. I'm flesh and blood, not like you, all piano wire and whipcord."

For him as for me, but for different reasons, 1923 was going to be a decisive year. In June, I had to tackle the School Certificate.

Hugh, older than I was, would have the Higher School Certificate to hurdle. Brilliant in maths, he was confident of taking it easily. He was looking beyond the H.S.C. He knew where he was going as well as he knew his way over the moors.

Only when we stopped for sandwiches could I keep pace with his talking. The hard going had been hard on my lungs, impaired a bit by pneumonia.

"Cambridge," said Hugh. "If I'm lucky, first class honours. Second will do. Then I can take my pick of the Civil Service jobs. The Chinese Secretariat in Kuala Lumpur . . . that's the job for me. Spend the first four years learning Chinese and the ways of the Chinese and Malays. Then six months home leave and I could go back as a Resident Magistrate and really begin to learn what life is all about. As Somerset Maugham learned it."

"Cambridge?" I said.

Hugh's dreams were not my dreams.

"Oxford for me. If only I can get matric. Your strong point is my weakest. Know how some fishermen cram maggots in their mouths? Ugh. That's what I feel like whenever I think of maths. But I must get matric. I must. If I don't get it at School Certif. level, I haven't an earthly at the advanced level."

"You'll get it," said Hugh.

A shock was in store for the whole of Crossleys when we returned after Easter.

In those days there were no Whitsuntide hols, only two days for the school sports. They were no sooner over than Woody, the maths master detonated his bombshell.

F. J. Woodhead had been a cowboy in Texas, a coffee planter in Brazil. So rumour asserted. He had come to Crossleys the term before to teach maths. Woody had new, refreshing ideas. He persuaded the headmaster. He got round the headmistress, the austere Miss Dale.

The Chairman of the Board of Governors was Halifax's M.P., Mr. Speaker Whitley. When he agreed to Wood-head's wild-and-woolly-West idea, the board agreed.

Crossleys was to go co-educational.

There was a broad aisle down the middle of dining hall, dividing the boys from the girls.

At the ding-dong clamour of the breakfast bell, we marched in from the left, the girls from the right.

We sounded like what we were, cheerful, rowdy, hungry animals.

On co-education morning, not knowing what to expect, we trooped in very quietly. There was no dividing aisle. Our tables and theirs had come together. Woody had arranged matters mathematically. From the top end where the sixth-formers sat, to the bottom end where the small fry were. We sat down side by side, boy, girl, boy, girl. We all looked at our plates and eyed each other sideways.

Normally, bold boys with roving eyes, eyed girls demure or provocative and flipped breadcrumbs across the gap, some of them wrapped in cheeky *billet-doux*.

Shy boys, longing to be as audacious, hadn't the nerve.

On co-education morning the mere physical closeness of boy sitting next to girl divided them by its stress as the aisle never had done.

As always, the head prefect on the boys' side stood up to say grace before the meal. "For what we are about to receive may the Lord make us truly thankful."

Silence for one fleeting moment and the usual zoo feeding noises burst out the louder for the restraint.

I ignored the girl on my deaf side and said to my neighbour on the right, "My name's Ronald Scriven. What's yours?"

"Monica Hainsworth."

How *did* one talk to girls?

An idea from nowhere flew into my head. I asked,

"Are you interested in birds' eggs?"

"Not very."

"My brother Neville is. You know him, don't you?"

"Yes," said Monica.

"We were both brought up on a farm. I was very keen on collecting birds' eggs. I'm not now, of course. I gave the lot to Neville. I used to keep the eggs in a toffee tin lined with cotton wool. Quite a good collection. I got two meadow pippits, a nuthatch and a nightjar."

"Oh?"

I went on talking to Monica, I could tell she was interested, she wasn't eating, she was looking at me.

"The colours and the spots and the sploshes," I explained to her "are for camouflage. That's why the cuckoo is so clever. She lays eggs in the nests of other birds when they're not looking. And the eggs she lays imitate the marking of say, a blackbird or a thrush. I once found a cuckoo's egg in the nest of a lesser spotted woodpecker."

The girls' head prefect, Bessie Parrot, stood up to say grace after the meal.

I didn't see her stand up because I was intent on talking to Monica and didn't hear what she said because I was deaf.

For a fleeting moment the dove of silence folded her wings. And I went on, at the top of my squawky lead-pencil voice instructing Monica how to distinguish the eggs of a bald-headed coot from those of a grebe. The whole school listened in silent rapture.

Neville yelled at me, "Shut up, Ron, you cuckoo."

Being male, I blamed the female for that awful moment.

For days afterwards I had my leg pulled, I was taunted and mocked, especially by Neville and his pestilential

152

friends Pip Musther and Co., jeering at me. Shouting, "Tweet, tweet. Are you interested in birds' eggs, Monica?"

Passionately, Pip rolled up his eyes and squawked, "Would you recognise the mating call of the corncrake, Monica?"

"Only if *you* made it to me, Ronald," piped Horrocks.

"Tweet, tweet," they circled round me, their arms flapping like wings.

"Can you hoot like a coot, Monica?"

In the dining hall, the girls made far more convincing bird calls to Monica.

Presently my fellow prefects put a stop to it.

I swotted and went on swotting for the coming exam.

The night before I had to face it, Bill Fox put his hand on my shoulder. "This won't do, old son. Ease up, or you'll flunk it. Come on. Let's go to Skircoat Green Library."

I took the exams.

In my favourite subjects I felt I'd done well but with maths and stinks and French to face, I was sure I hadn't done well enough. When I handed in my final paper, I was certain the examiners would plough me.

We stayed at Ellers Road for a weekend with Grandma Scriven and Aunt Jess. Then we went off to South Milford. Half way through the hols we were switched abruptly to stay with Uncle James and Aunt Florence in their new bungalow at Huby.

James had had it built against his retirement a few years ahead. Moorlands, in half an acre of land cut out from the intake, a bite taken out of the moor. The bungalow overlooking the valley of the lower Wharfe was beautiful. James had arranged for the long rustic summerhouse from the bottom of his garden in Francis

Street to be transplanted and rebuilt at the side of the new bungalow.

From the summerhouse corner I could see Low Moor farm down in the valley with the familiar whaleback of Wearybones Hill behind it. Strangers now farmed Low Moor.

On Saturday mornings James liked to breakfast in the summerhouse. Pink out of a hot bath, pyjamaed, and robed in a camelhair dressing gown he joined us to preside over breakfast.

Old-fashioned, he said grace before meat, as we did at Crossleys. His silver hair ruffled, he clasped his hands, closed his eyes and said, "For what we are about to receive, may the Lord make us truly thankful." In the same tone and in the same breath as he lifted the silver cover from the dish, he added, "Dammit, the bacon's cold."

I'd rather have been at Milford, but it didn't really matter where I was. In August the results of the School Certificate would be published. It was enough, meanwhile, to steer as clear as I could from irritating James.

Kindly, voluble Aunt Florence had one battle cry. "Don't cross your uncle."

One morning she said, "Ronald. Mrs. Robinson is ill in Otley Cottage Hospital. I'm sure you'd like to visit her. I'll cut a big bunch of flowers for you. You can get to Otley by bus from the bottom of Huby Hill." I didn't want to go, but I went.

It was quite a long walk from Otley market square to the hospital. I didn't like the look of the place. It was a low, rambling building of grey stone. It looked as I had seen many rows of terrace houses look. As though they had been positioned so that the sun could shine on them but never go in. Not even through the closed windows.

The stiff-starched nurse who asked my business directed me.

Inside the hospital the air had the sick-sour smell of old people and disinfectant. I found the ward.

She was in the last bed. I pulled up a chair and sat beside her. I thought she was asleep. Her hair, which I so well remembered being scraped back and screwed into a tight bun, was loose on her shoulders.

God. I remembered how she would put on a fresh apron before even the postman saw her. I laid the flowers on the bed. Ann opened her eyes. How often, how often had she looked at me over the top of her steel-rimmed specs, but not with eyes faded now as the blue-print blouse she used to wear. Her fingers moved over the quilt. Still work-worn hard, her hand felt thin and dry.

"How are you, Ann?" I asked her.

"Nobbut middlin'."

Searching my mind for something to say I remembered what Mrs. Church had told me a year or so ago.

"I heard you went to Canada to see your son, John."

"So ah did. 'E sent mi t' money for t' fare. Six months ah stayed wi' 'im an' 'is fam'ly."

"Whatever did you come back for?"

"Ah'd seen 'im. It were enough," was all she said.

I knew Ann then in a way I had never known her. I gave her hand a squeeze.

"Go on wi thi," I said, "Tha's a reight Yorkshire lass, tha'd ev nowt to do wi them Canada fowk and their daft ways."

From out of the centre of her milky-rimmed eyes flew a spark of the still warm fire of Ann's pride.

"Tha's reet," she said.

A burning feeling of anger totally unexpected . . .

surprising, rose from my belly to my mouth. Anger at whatever had brought her to this hateful, poverty-stinking place.

Frustration followed anger that there was no way I could do what I ached to do. To pick her up and set her back in time in her own kitchen at Low Moor in the place where she belonged.

Pharoah, Pharoah. "What happened to Pharoah, Ann?"

"He de'ed a two-three month afore Joe."

When I got up to leave she said, "Tell thi brother I asked after him. Tha'll none be coming to see me agen."

I looked at her. I knew, suddenly, that I loved her. Deliberately I paid her back in her own iron coin.

I said: "Nay lass, yer not goin' to dee yet."

Ann cackled with glee. She laughed so much that the death rattle almost took her by the throat.

"I'll fetch it, Uncle." Neville was up and off.

The half-made garden, the bright morning, the spurt and clear flame of the wax Vesta my uncle held to the end of his cigar, all seemed to become abruptly dulled, as though a cloud had passed across the sun.

The exams.

I saw Neville pounding up the drive.

I *had* failed.

Neville shouted, "Ron, Ron. You've done it. You've got matric. Told you you would."

Matric. The magic word shouted everything else out of my head.

Matriculation meant that I'd be let off the otherwise compulsory entrance exam for Oxford. Matric. I'd done it. I'd got it. Oxford. Oxford. Oxford.

Uncle James astounded me out of my incredulity. He pulled a quid out of his pocket. "Congratulations. I'm very pleased, Ronald. This calls for a celebration. Florence, pack the picnic hamper."

He glanced authoritatively at the sky, "The day's going to come out fine and sunny. We'll spend it by the sea. Ronald, go and help your aunt. Neville, get the swimming togs and towels. Be ready when I bring the Sunbeam round."

Aunt Florence was rushing round the kitchen. "How your Uncle expects me to get everything ready while he just fetches the car, I don't know. And where are we going anyway?"

"Where would you like to go, Aunt Florence?"

"Oh, Robin Hood's Bay. I love it. It's so bracing. I'd always hoped your uncle would have bought one of those lovely cottages there for his retirement. Where's the Gentleman's Relish. Oh, dear, I forgot it last time. There's your uncle blowing his horn."

As we scrambled into the back seat, Neville asked, "Where are we going, Uncle?"

"Bridlington."

I said "Aunt Florence wants to go to . . . "

Aunt Florence said quickly, "Don't cross your uncle, Ronald."

The big, twenty-horsepower Sunbeam, built more like a yacht than a car, cruised past the crowded harbour of the old town, the hotels, and headed south.

"Your uncle," said Florence, "hates charabancs and trippers."

About five miles south on the coast road, Uncle swung the Sunbeam between a gap in the dunes and on to the low, shelving sands, which stretched for miles. Not a charabanc, not a tripper, not a soul.

Floating blissfully in the sea, looking up at the sky I saw a complete circular rainbow round the sun. The rings were faint and very beautiful. A gull was shouting. "Kitty-wake, Kittywake."

I watched it swoop and dive. Then the sky was empty blueness except for the sun and the rainbow.

My legs were abruptly dragged down and I went under. I surfaced angrily. Neville, the better swimmer, had ducked me for the fun of it. He struck out for the shore and I chased him over the hard-ribbed sand.

"Pax," he gasped.

We sat lazily and looked out to sea for Uncle James. There was nothing in sight. "Drowned himself," said Neville.

James, as we both knew, was a very powerful swimmer. Then I spotted him. He was making capital headway for the Dutch coast. Presently he turned and swam back. We watched him splashing towards us. He looked massive in his horizontally striped red-and-yellow bathing costume.

Neville was choking himself laughing. "He's like a b'b'balloon that's come down in the s'sea."

I'd meant to mention to Neville the circular rainbow round the sun but it went and I forgot it.

The only thing that upset James about the picnic was that Aunt Florence had forgotten mustard.

His after-lunch cigar soothed him.

Aunt Florence said, "Now you're all satisfied, I'm taking off my shoes and going for a paddle." She went off on her own which was what she wanted to do.

James looked at us. "Take your bucket, Neville, and find some good white pebbles for the garden."

"Righty-ho. Coming, Ron?"

"You stay with me, Ronald. I want to talk to you."

I thought Oh, Lord. Here it comes.

"Now you've done so well in your exams the time has

come to consider your future. Have you given the matter any thought?"

"Of course I have, Uncle. Oxford first and then I want to be a writer."

When James said "H'rrumph," I knew I'd said something to cross him. I fell silent. What *was* the matter with him? I knew he was a straight-from-the-shoulder man. He'd give an honest answer and he'd expect an honest answer. Yet time and again when I'd given him just that, he was either vexed or furious with me. Why? I nearly asked him there and then. He'd asked for a straight answer and I'd given him one. Fred's favourite word came into my mind. 'Heck.' What did he want me to say? What did he want me to do? What was he going to say? What was he going to do?

James drew on his cigar. I knew by his eyes that he was thinking. He said, "You want to be a writer, Ronald? You're sixteen. What do you know about writing at your age? It's not my line. I'm an engineer. Like your father and my father before me. But I know this much about it, you can't write — nobody can write until they've had some experience of life. What experience of life have you had? None."

I wanted to burst out, I wanted to say, 'Plenty'. I didn't. What was the use of trying to tell him all I'd been through with Iron Ann, with my deafness? No use at all. He wouldn't understand.

Looking back on it now, I can see that we were at complete cross-purposes. When he told me that I couldn't become a writer until I had experienced life, he had hit the wrong nail bang on the head. He'd told me the truth about writing. Yes. He hadn't told me, what he clearly realised and I didn't, that in order to write, or do anything else, one must stay alive. Stand on one's feet and earn one's living. And what chance had a deaf boy to do that?

James was thoroughly perplexed.

In the early twenties England was sliding into the depression. As my guardian, James was responsible for looking after me. Not to mention looking after Neville.

There was plenty of money available to look after both of us. Our patrimony administered by James. And there was I, wanting to go to Oxford. What on earth, James asked himself, was the use of sending a deaf boy to Oxford? No, a sheer waste of money.

And how could I then, saying to myself 'Heck', have understood what was passing through my uncle's mind?

James pressed the stub of his cigar into the sand. He'd made up his mind. All his cautious conservative instincts, as hindsight tells me, had urged him to do what he did do. Compromise. He said, "Ronald, whether you go to Oxford or not, you'll have to wait a couple of years before that decision is reached. In the meanwhile, you will go back to Crossleys."

The pi-jaw was over. For two wonderful years I stayed on at Crossleys. Nobody cared what I did or didn't do. Newport was pleased with me. By taking matric at sixteen, I'd notched one more success in the school's academic record. All he said was, "You scraped through in maths by two marks." He knew and I knew that he knew that Crossleys had done all it could do for my formal education. No point in my going through the motions of continuing it further in class. I had *carte blanche* to do as I pleased.

Robb waylaid me. "You've got a golden chance to catch up with your real education. Grab it with both hands."

I grabbed my golden years and devoured them. With-

out a care in the world about exams, I wolfed them at
school.

My holidays at Ellers Road, at Milford, at Huby were
heart's delight. Especially at Milford, where in summer
I roamed field and wood and footpath at one with them
all, with the briar which twitched at my sleeve from the
greensleeves hedge, with the lark whose song I could not
hear, with the flower-enamelled meadows and the
hunting weasel which whipped across my path.

Sometimes Neville came with me. More often I was
out on my own.

I knew Milford for what it was. The most ordinary,
the flattest, the most humdrum of all the villages on the
flat edge of the Vale of York. As it was also what
Caxton, when he Englished *The Golden Legend of The
Lives of the Saints*, called 'Fore to the Gates of Paradise.'

Yet it was in Huby, a village I never learned to love,
that I had the nearest thing I had encountered to a
mystical experience at Riffa Wood. A paved footpath
went through that wood. The stones had once been a
Roman chariot way. In spring, in bluebell time, I went
that way.

The wood was very still. An oak spread its branches
across the path. I sensed something deep and primitive
in it, drawing me to it as to something holy. I clasped
the trunk with my arms. My feet stirred the leaf-mould
of many a summer. I felt as though my feet were
joining the roots of the tree. Digging deep, deep drawing
sap from the earth. Drawing the lifesap up, up into the
tree that was one with my body. Up to the branches to
the twigs, the leaves, sap rising to the tree's flowering,
which in springtime must happen before the fruit is
formed and the seed which renews the life of the tree.

I pressed my fingertips into the crannies of the bark.

In a kind of oneness I felt the sap rise, the pulsing of my own blood through my fingertips. I knew the moment of ecstasy, the standing apart from the body. My body and the body of the tree seemed to me to be one and not one. Between one ·heartbeat and the next I had known mystic experience which has its being outside time and in eternity. And in that timeless communion was at one with that universal nature in which we both had our roots.

So, in my two golden years, I passed through the wood of dreams and, in passing, brushed, who knows, against ultimate reality.

In the nearest thing on earth to the garden of Eden, that is to say, childhood, I had become aware of the tree of the knowledge of good and of evil. In Riffa Wood, I believe I touched the tree God forbade Adam to touch — the tree of life.

Chapter 14

BEDLAM

In Riffa Wood the April dusk was deepening. Cuckoo
. . . cuckoo. The floating notes blended with the faint
blue woodsmoke haze of twilight drifting through the
trees. A filament of spider silk touched my cheek. As I
put up my hand, I sensed its physical warmth. I thought,
if that were a briar and scratched my skin my blood
would smell of the violet. Oh, Christ, it's spring. Spring,
and I ought to be in Wensleydale with Rose. Instead, I
had been ordered to visit Uncle James.

At the top of the woodland ride night was drinking
from her tilted cup the last lees of day.

I sauntered up the hill to the bungalow.

"Come in, Ronald," said Aunt Florence, "Your uncle
wants to see you. I've held back dinner half-an-hour as it
is and you know what he's like at the best of times."

She nudged my elbow in the hall. "Don't cross your
uncle."

James, a simmering thundercloud, did not speak for a
moment. Then, "You're late. Sit down. You can hear
me, I suppose?"

163

"Yes."

"You were nineteen last Wednesday."

"Correct."

"Don't use that tone to me."

He sat with his knees wide apart. A large hand on each. I saw that the veins on the back of his hands were prominent.

"I have given you a fair crack of the whip. You left Crossleys last October. As far as I can gather you spend your days idling about. It's time you told me what you propose to do."

I looked at him. "I have already told you. I want to be a writer." The antagonism between us flared up. Heedless of Aunt Florence's warning I added recklessly, "A poet."

The thundercloud clapped.

"Who do you think you are, Shakespeare?"

"Of course not. I have never called myself a poet out loud to scarcely anyone before. You asked me what I wanted to do, I told you, I want to write poetry."

There were books within James's reach. For an instant I thought he was going to do what he had once done when he was giving me a wigging, and I was holding an open book and pretending not to hear him. Then, James had snatched the book out of my grasp, thrown it to the floor and stamped on it in lieu of giving me a thrashing.

I was not afraid of him. He had never raised his hand to me in all the years he had been my guardian. It did not occur to me that *his* sense of justice was outraged.

After a minute or two he said, "That's enough. I told you I would give you six months to find a job on your own. On a newspaper, in a library, anything that would give you any kind of footing. I told you, your aunt and I would be happy for you to live here until such time as

164

you could wholly support yourself. Are you going to tell me you've found a publisher for your poetry?"

"No."

"Very well, then. You will start in the machine shop your grandfather founded. I shall arrange for you to lodge with one of our charge-hands. I have already sounded Herbert Boardman on the matter."

Words started stumbling from my mind to my mouth. To tell him I had had my bellyful of his arrangements. Tell him that Robb had sent a poem of mine to J. C. Squire of *The London Mercury*, who had liked it.

"You'll clock in on Monday morning."

James rose and dismissed me as though I were already at the works.

On Monday morning James caught a far earlier train than usual. As the slow-snorting engine quickened its breath of steam, James snorted. "Stop fidgeting." The raw-stiff overalls chafed my wrists and neck. The uniform of a convict. Bound not for Dartmoor, but the works. James lit a cigar. Christ, I thought. He hasn't a clue.

The immense doors of the main machine shop had been partly pulled open on their rollers. Roaring, grinding, screaming bedlam belched out of them as we passed. My deafness was no more a barrier against that tidal wave of sound than a bathing dress would have been a protection against a tidal wave of water.

Shattered, I followed James through the office entrance and up flights of concrete stairs.

In his own office, James was a person I had never seen before. He put on authority as he hung up his jacket. A man with a nearly white coat and an almost square head came in.

"Bob, this is my nephew Ronald. Bob Fieldhouse is

our machine foreman. Your own immediate boss will be the charge-hand, Herbert Boardman. The dinner whistle goes at twelve noon. You'll lunch with me in the board room."

"Where do the men lunch, Uncle?"

Bob Fieldhouse said, "They don't lunch. They bring snap-tins. If it's none raining, they squat on t' pavement in York Street."

"I'll eat with the men, Uncle."

"Please yourself. But you'd better lunch with me today."

"No thanks. I won't bother with lunch. I'll begin as I mean to go on."

In bedlam itself the pandemoniacal clamour was mitigated by the sight of what was going on in hell. Blue overalled slaves gave monstrous, battleship-grey machines their food — steel.

So high overhead that it was just beneath the long, long rows of skylights, a travelling crane carried to the larger monsters, lumps of steel too heavy to be manhandled.

Well below the level of the travelling crane, shafting lined each side of the great central bay. Endless loops of leather belting, some tight, some slack, linked the main shafting to this or that grey monster.

The immense din confused, the moving monsters confounded and the linking belts made my head spin. Into my spinning head, dived thought. This, this had been my father's world.

Clangour beat with Titan fists against my eardrums, my temples. Mysterious, uncomprehended movement dizzied my sight.

A line of Kit Marlowe's was thrown to me like a life-line by memory:

'And this is hell, nor am I out of it.'

A human voice shouted close to my better ear. "This is Herbert Boardman. He's gaffer over thee."

Solid, stolid, the charge-hand shook hands. Herbert's palm pressed against mine, not sweat but sump oil. My first contact with the greasy, pore-clogging stuff no scrubbing of soap and water could cleanse from the skin for long.

"Come wi' me, lad." From silent films *The Perils of Pauline* and *The Four Horsemen of the Apocalypse*, I had picked up, because of my deafness, a bit of lip-reading. I read Herbert's easily, for as I was to learn he was a man of few and short words.

"This machine is a shaper. Lad working it is Bill Watson. He'll larn thee."

The shaper was a small, chunky monstrosity. Bill Watson was chunky. He was flesh and blood all right and smiled, not with his eyes. They looked at me as I had looked at the monstrosity, which was jabbing away at a gobbet of steel clamped in front of it. Bill said "You've never worked with them 'ands. I've addled me livin' wi' mine ever since I left schooil. T' week after I wor twelve."

"Addled?"

"Earned," said Bill. He smiled with his eyes this time. With a rare flash of understanding of a stranger, I guessed that my utter ignorance had made him feel a bit superior.

I got the hang of the shaper. Its cutting tool pared from the gobbet of steel, stroke by stroke, a shaving of metal. By the time the cutting tool had finished with it, the gobbet was mirror-smooth. Bill unclamped the steel and put in the vice another, caked with the black furnace-sand in which it had been rough-cast. Stroke by stroke, it pared that, too, mirror-smooth.

167

The great gas engine, with a driving wheel thirteen foot in diameter, sang its deep, diapason song: THUT THUT THUT, THUTTER THUT THUT THUTTER THUT as it drove the shafting on each side of the machine-shop's bay.

As the morning wore on, I realised that the shaper's sole function was to pare into smoothness these pieces of blistered metal.

A high-pitched whistle cut through the bedlam of noise as the shaper's tool cut through the steel.

Silence came with something like the shock of clangour.

"Hasta gottn thi snap-tin?" asked Bill. "Noa? I'll share mine wi' thee."

I sat on the pavement beside him, unable to squat on my hunkers as they did.

From left and right men and boys kept on looking at me.

The whistle blew again, its piercing note muffled almost at once by the THUT THUT THUT THUTTER THUT of the gas engine.

At half past five the engine slowed, the belts went slack, the wheels ran down and quietness suddenly flowed above the stilled machines arrested now at quarter stroke.

Mechanics stripped their jackets off and washed their arms to the elbow-joints in thick green oil with dull, flat sheens. Then slapping cap or trilby on, streamed through the great doors and were gone.

Herbert and I set off together. When we got off the tram, he took me through short, narrow, cobbled streets whose names proclaimed their spawning: Inkerman Street; Balaclava Road; Crimea Mount. We passed grimed, monotonous brick-built back-to-back houses.

168

Each house in an almost identical street, each house one-and-a-scullery down, one-and-a-cramped-bedroom up.

"Sebastopol Street," Herbert said, "Number Three." And there it was, two steps up, open the door and we were inside.

"The missus."

We both took off our caps.

Flo Boardman took both my hands. In Flo's slender, frail-seeming hand my own hands felt a joyous spirit making its presence known. Herbert took me into the scullery and teemed into the brown stone sink a ladle full of steaming water from the kitchen hob. We scrubbed ourselves. But not clean. Almost as soon as I had dried myself oil began to make my skin feel greasy again.

"Come to table, Ronald. Herbert and I have never had a lodger before. You'll be a bit of company for him. He doesn't talk much, my Herbert, but he listens."

"Aye," said Herbert.

A shutter deep in my being opened and closed like the lense of a camera. These two, I realised in its flash, loved each other in the way my father and mother had been in love.

Going to the table was easy in that cribb'd and cabin'd room. One stride from the scullery door. There were only two chairs, Herbert's with a blue and white ringed pint pot to his right on the white cloth spread over a green plush one.

"Surely, I'm taking your chair, Mrs. Boardman?" Flo laughed softly.

"Nay, Ronald. I sit down sometimes and put my feet up. I'm not wanting anything just now. Tea is my weakness. I'd lose count if I bothered to. You can have a pint pot if you like but I reckon you'd want a cup and saucer, like me. Ee, what am I doing chattering away like a budgie?"

She squeezed past Herbert, a square of harding in her hand. As the oven door opened, a rich waft of smell suffused the air.

"Careful, love, the plate's hot."

Herbert's knife and fork were standing to attention when she set his helping before him.

The table was as crowded with lesser dishes as the kitchen was with Gosse china knick-knacks.

As we ate, Flo sang away like a canary hopping inconsequentially from branch to branch in an aviary.

"The milkman shut his can as soon as he'd ladled a gill into the jug. He'd forgotten I ordered an extra pint. Mrs. Mester borrowed a gill and I had to send Annie round to the dairy. Poor Annie, her dad's been laid off again. If one kid knocked at my door wanting a jam jar to get into the matinee at the pictures, a baker's dozen did. There weren't no cinema when you and me was kids, was there, Herbert?"

"Aye," said Herbert, through a mouthful of ham.

"Listen to him, Ronald. When he's eating my Herbert just guesses by the tone of my voice whether to say yes or no."

"Aye," said Herbert.

"The coalman turned up this afternoon. He wouldn't let Mrs. Rogers have even a quarter of a sack because Sam Rogers has been out of a job since the new year. And her expecting again. So I went round with a scuttlefull soon's the coal cart turned into Balaclava Mount. Nay, it makes me ashamed with us so well off and all. My Herbert's never been off work for a day since we were married and him a charge hand this last five years."

Late April dusk let fall over the day the skyfall of her hair.

"Light the gas for me, Herbert, love. There, that's more like. Now I'll clear the table and wash up."

"Let me, Mrs. Boardman. I am a dab hand at it. Ann . . . oh, you don't know about her. When I was ten I had to wash up and dry after a farmhouse meal."

"Nay, love. I always like the table set and ready for breakfast. You have a bit of a chat with Herbert. He'll tell you owt you want to know about cricket."

"But I don't . . . " I bit my tongue.

I need not have done. The word 'cricket' unlocked Herbert's lips and freed the prisoner, speech.

He was changing overs and setting the field for a left-hander when someone knocked, and the door opened. Flo came out of the scullery.

"Come in, Mrs. Mester."

"Sorry. I'd forgotten you'd a lodger now. It's about Mr. Mester. I popped his Sunday boots this morning, not thinking on it's his lodge night at t' Buff'lo's. I wondered if . . . . "

"I can lend you a florin if you promise to pay it back on pay day."

"Could you make it half a crown, Flo?"

She was fat, and I liked neither her looks nor the wheezy, whining intonation of her speech.

Flo took her purse from the niche between the aspidistra and the only book in the house, the Bible.

"She's had a hard life," said Flo and began to relay the table.

"Many's the time Mrs. Mester has to make do with a York Road tablecloth. That's a newspaper, love. Herbert, show Ronald his bedroom."

The stairs weren't much wider than Herbert's

shoulders. My bedroom was so narrow that I could touch the walls either side of the bed. Between the top and foot of that bed was about half a yard of freeboard. An arc light, slung on cross-wires at the corner of Sebastopol Street, swung up and down. As it swung up, lurid light swilled over the wallpaper patterned like the China vases in the kitchen, with cabbage roses. When the shade dipped, a shadow like the wing of a vulture obliterated the roses on the opposite wall.

Herbert lit a candle. Its milk light, made fitful by the arc lamp, showed me that the floor was uneven and covered by scrupulously clean linoleum. Pillow, sheets, wincey blankets were as Dutch-clean. I did not have to guess by whose hands. The upper sash was down a few inches. Through it came a sour smell.

Herbert blew out the candle.

"What would you like to do on your first evening, love?" asked Flo.

"Herbert doesn't drink but he'll take you out to the Tulip in Cherry Row if you like, or the Eagle in York Road."

"I don't drink, Mrs. Boardman."

She touched my sleeve. "Call me Flo. Everybody does. What would you like to do, then?"

I hesitated.

"Go to the pictures?" She read the answer in my eyes. "Tell me then. Whatever it is."

"Honestly? Very well. I want to write."

"A letter to your girl? We've got some note paper somewhere."

I made my eyes blank. "No."

I looked away, not liking to lie to her. Rose of all roses, Rose of Wensleydale.

"I've got lashings of writing paper. If I could have a

172

corner of the table . . . . "

Everything that had happened to me since I had been pitchforked into the insane maelstrom of the works and dragged out of its vortex to be flung into this brickwork jungle swirled within me, like whirls of nebulous gas round a world in the making light-years away in space. Ideas, images, thoughts, emotions . . . all churned me into a fine, creative fury.

Within ten days Flo had demolished defences I had made, I thought, rock-fast after my father's death.

I lived in the kind of loneliness I did not even suspect is fundamentally the loneliness of all mankind.

I was a stranger and afraid — as Housman said — in a world I never made.

Now I found myself in a prison within a prison. Neither in the brick jungle nor, still less, in the works could I hope to find any who spoke my language.

Night after night, high tea over, I wrote and read.

I had discovered Masefield.

I have seen dawn and sunset on moor and windy hills,
Coming in solemn beauty like slow old tunes of Spain.
I have seen the lady April,
Bringing the daffodils . . . .

Not to the demented bedlam of the works. And to the brick-jumble-sad blades of grass soon wilting like the children of that dreadful wilderness.

In the works a spirit other than that of spring was troubling me. Wrapped up in my own inner world and because I had no idea of what was normal in the machine shop, how could I sense what was astir?

Normality I had come to equate with George Padgett, the shop steward who could not utter a sentence without using the Army's favourite word at least three times.

Bedlam still shrieked and screamed. The din, though

infernal, had taken on the quality of mad music orchestrated by some tortured soul in hell. THUT THUT THUT THUTTER THUT roared the great gas-engine. Naysmith hammers in the next bay, the welding shop pounded contrapuntally. They could flatten chunks of steel six inches thick or, at the whim of their users, just brush the bloom from a butterfly's wing.

"We are the borers. Hear us bore," ground the vertical milling machines.

Ten feet away from the shaper I was supposed to operate on my own a small battery of emery wheels that spat sparks like miniature comets. Nearby were two power-driven grindstones for sharpening cutting-tools blunted by the first coat of sand-blistered steel ingots.

My head no longer ached from the hell-reverberating pandemonium.

George Padgett put a new edge on the tungsten-tipped cutter of his plate-edge planer and came to shout at me.

"Flicker it, there's going to be a fluctuating strike. The flashing miners won't freezingly stand it another flamboyant day. Flatulate the flaming Duke o' Northumberland. A. J. Cook's phosphorescently well stirred 'em out."

At half past five the engine slowed, the belts went slack, the wheels ran down.

Herbert said his Yorkshireman's say — nowt — all the way to Sebastopol Street.

"What's up, love?" asked Flo.

George Padgett yelled the answer next morning. He could be heard all over the machine shop, for the belt of the gas-engine had broken.

"Down fascinating tools. THE GENERAL FLUSHING STRIKE'S ON. One out, all fornicating out."

Half the men had not even hung up their cloth caps.

As I turned joyfully to join the exodus Bob Fieldhouse, the foreman, intercepted me.

"Where do you think you're goin'? To t' pictures?"

"I'm joining the men of course."

"You must be wrong in your bloody head. Apprentices are neutral. Strikers don't want em. No more than't bosses do. And I'm one o' t' bosses."

Bob, grinning, shepherded the mutinous machine-shop lads into the huge yard at the back of the works. The day before, fifty tons of coal from the Lady Pit had been delivered. Bob handed out shovels.

"Tha sees yon coal. Shift it fro' *theer* t' *theer*."

That was on the 8th of May.

Each of the few days the strike lasted the machine-shop apprentices passed through the jeering picket lines, all of us sullen.

"I'm all for the strikers," I told Flo. "I'd man the barricades with them if I could. The works, these back-to-backs, have opened my eyes to what goes on. What chance have the workers ever had? They're half starved, poor devils."

"I know, love," said Flo. She picked up her square of harding and squeezed past Herbert.

"Fynnon haddock, with a poached egg on top. I've not used as much milk as I'd have liked."

I glanced at her quickly. I knew by now that she kept herself going on cups of tea and odds and sods of bread and jam and the like.

"I'm not very hungry."

"Might as well talk to yon brick wall, lad," said Herbert. "Eat your tea, like me. You're t' only breadwinner now."

The general strike was broken in eleven days. It took three months to starve the miners back into the pits at wages less than those against which they'd struck.

Chapter 15

MONKEY PARADE

Heat breathed over the back-to-backs so stiflingly that their brickwork panted back a foetid jungle smell. Men's faces were grey-greasy, like their cloth caps. Wages drawn on Saturday morning before the strike had tided some of them partly over the first week of it. Hundreds of families had lived hand to mouth before it started, their breadwinners on short time. Pawnbrokers and betting shops held the keys of that dreary kingdom of despairing.

Now the strike was over, those lucky enough to be taken on again would have to wait a further week for depleted wage packets to perform their pitiable miracles.

"We'd have managed, Herbert and me," said Flo. "He's gotten a bit put by for a rainy day, but there are that many with nothing and less than nothing."

She brightened.

"When you've washed yourselves there's something ready for both of you. Come Saturday, Herbert'll be drawing his wages again. Then I can make up for some of the things you've gone short of. And happen a bit more."

"Short? You've done me proud."

"Is that what you think? You haven't eyes in your head, love. Nay, I've tried to make up for giving you 'maggy-ann' instead of best butter but I've been right ashamed, with your twenty-five bob a week coming in."

"You've darned my socks, sewn my shirt buttons on, washed my filthy overalls. Good lord, I've been ashamed to hold out my hand for my pay packet."

There was a rat-tat-tatting at the door. A noise that sounded like the arrival of a posse of police. It was one small boy. He held out to Flo in a grubby fist a bunch of wilting bluebells.

"Bless you, Johnny," said Flo.

The boy mumbled himself away.

"They're starved for flowers as well as food. He must have walked four mile to pick them. Lots of them round here bring me wild flowers. They're the kids I save my jam jars for. The rag-and-bone man gives them a copper or two if they can give him enough jars."

After the meal I cleared my writing corner.

"Eeeee," said Flo. "Do you write on and on like this at your uncle's the doctor in South Milford? It can't be good for you stopping indoors all the time. It gives *me* a bit of a headache and I'm used to it. Why not go out for a walk for a change, love."

I pushed my work away.

"To please my guardian angel, I will."

Sebastopol Street. Balaclava Road. A pawnbroker's with three gold balls from the coat of arms of the Medici proclaimed the origin of its trade. 'Uncle' would remain open late into the night. Crimea Mount. Despite the heatwave stench, the rows of back-to-backs were not crowded. I was stalking among ghosts. Ghosts older than those of the Light Brigade haunted hereabouts. Primrose

Hill. Lavender Walk. Green Road.

I sauntered its grimy pavement thinking, the just-living mingled now with the shades. Aimlessness, which had guided, deserted me. I would make my way to the other side of town. To Ellers Road and see my Grandma. A corner. A second corner and York Road. The windows of a famous local pub, the Woodpecker, offended the late May daylight with garish lights. Now there were people as well as a flowing traffic stream of horses and carts, cabs, traps and now and then motor cars.

A man's shoulder butted me, Yorkshire fashion, a quarter-circle sideways. The heedless impact annoyed me and changed my mood. I swung on my heel and went, not down York Road, townwards, but up. There the great arterial-traffic river cut its way through the densest mile of the city.

Footsteps were loud on the pavement. Footsteps on both banks of the traffic stream, blending with the sound of it, making that sound deeper and somehow alive. The footsteps were made by groups of boys and girls. The boys walked in pairs, or in threes with now and then near the entrance of a pub a group which could become the nucleus of a gang.

The girls walked in couples. Tailoresses, seamstresses, buttonholers employed by the big multiple clothing factories. Some were what Herbert would call buxom lasses. Some thin, stoop-shouldered, pale, who seemed to have put all their strength into growing their hair.

Up and down, between the Woodpecker and the Hope, the sexes segregated, these youngsters of the slums roamed, before dusk, in the early stages of the monkey parade.

I had seen the monkey parade before, mostly through the windows of tram-cars. Something amusing about it had sent an old song from the Music Halls tripping into my head. I whistled:

I'm Burlington Bertie,
I rise at ten thirty.
I walk down the Strand
With my gloves on my hand
And I walk up again with them off.

As the almost coppery, heat-hazed sky began to fore-shadow the advent of dusk the parade too altered its nature. The rhythms of the traffic seemed to be intensi-fied, to pound and beat like drums. The shrill jabbering of the paraders changed its key. Three boys would challenge two girls with bantered words, part invitation, part insult, in a jargon I did not understand, a ritual I did not know, although I could not mistake the amorous quality of what was going on. A boy would pair with a girl, girl link arms with a boy and the odd boy out would hoot with laughter and become a lone hunter seeking a girl who had been left out on her own.

Light, fading from the sky, darkened to a deeper blue, as suddenly all the street lamps went on. A girl looked over her shoulder and called to me: "Does yer mother know yer out?"

The beat of the traffic stream became insistent, the beat of my own bloodstream drumming in my ears.

Now all the couples were going the same way: I guessed they did not want the last dregs of daylight in the sky nor the glare of street lamps. The other self, the one that talks to a man in his head, urged me; "Turn away. Go back to Flo's." All my instincts, save one, prompted me to do so.

I went with the tail end of the monkey parade.

An iron archway marked off from the interminable maze of back-to-backs a double terrace of better, stone-built properties. Houses of skilled, better-paid artisans: among them, as I knew, Bob Fieldhouse, the works foreman. This was East End Park Road. At its far end stood the rusted, gap-toothed railings of East End Park itself. No park rangers troubled, or perhaps dared, to patrol its scruffy wilderness of cinder tracks, shrubs and soot-choked trees. Here and there were backless benches, thick — and thick-grimed — planks. The monkey parade had almost vanished, dispersed into that wilderness. But I could hear monkeys about their monkey business. Behind me a girl's voice screamed;

"Don't you go with that Jack, our 'Ilda. He'll do yer."

My other self tapped my shoulder;

"You know what's going on in those shrubberies. You're no Peeping Tom. Get the hell out of this."

I kept to the main cinder track. The slope steepened. Ahead I saw a haze of coloured lights. Heard, in my better ear, a sound which moved me like music.

The park ended on the lip of a deep railway cutting. In its depth was a brilliantly lit, lone signal box. Neville Hill. Like random fireflies red or green lights floated. Lights that vanished, reappeared, changed places.

The loved music deepened, rhythmic, dragon-snorting. The 9.03 night passenger swept through the cutting, its nine coaches a dazzle of running light. My heartbeat quickened as its bogies clicked to the train's gathering speed. It would stop at Garforth . . . Micklefield . . . South Milford, where my heart but not my body would jump off.

For a long time I watched those fireflies. They clustered on gantries where the night goods were shunted in and out of Neville Hill marshalling yard. Once, the sultry air was freshened by an updraught as the sleeper for Newcastle rocked past spitting red sparks.

Moonlight. My shoes scuffled the cinder tracks. The

stink parched the back of my throat.

I had watched the train noisily taking luckier ones from the city to the stopping places of their homes. Flo and Herbert would be in bed by now. I had no latchkey, none was needed.

During the time I stayed in Sebastopol Street nobody ever locked their doors.

A light burned in the kitchen.

"Oh, Flo, you shouldn't have waited up for me," I said. "Go to bed. You must be tired out."

"Eeee, love, I'm past it. I'm a poor sleeper. You're not *that* late in. Did you have a nice walk?"

I sensed that she meant what she said. She was past tiredness. In less than a month, without direct speech, Flo had taught me more about herself than Iron Ann had in a year. Now I knew, when Flo pushed a tendril of hair with the back of her hand, that only the strength of her spirit kept her on the go.

She wanted to talk. In the small hours, in that small, cheerfully overcrowded room I told her about Low Moor and Ann's peacock, Pharoah, and how he had screamed that the thaw was to come the night Ann had told me of my parents' death. She touched my hand.

"I'm glad you told me, Ron, love. I can understand why you and your little brother were sent to live on a farm, what with the war and all. But *whatever* were your uncles and aunts thinking of to let such dreadful news be broken to you by that hard old woman in such a way?"

The pressure on my hand was as gentle, touch-healing as balm in Gilead.

Obliquely, I turned away from her hand of healing.

"You asked me, had I had a nice walk? I will tell you all about it. I walked through poverty and squalor I didn't believe existed outside the pages of Dickens a hundred years ago. I rubbed shoulders with . . . with . . ."

"I know, love. You won't offend me. Don't think badly of them. They're starved of such a lot, poor kids. Just starved of all the things young ones want, and a lot of them are starved of love. It isn't sin which makes them behave like they do. It's wilfulness. It's ignorance. And they're not all like that. It *would* be a world if they were. Eeee, look at the clock. You'll never be up for work in the morning."

Most nights of the next week or two I was writing what I thought to be good stuff. Then I became restless.

Herbert had scrubbed, changed, wolfed his tea and rushed out to umpire an evening cricket match. Flo was dying to talk and didn't. Restlessness drove my thought and my pen.

Defeat. Our trumpets sang for the foregone rally
bitter and gay and reckless. A hopeless token.
We knew the uselessness of sortie or sally,
knew that our case was lost, our ranks were broken,
disdaining to hoist on a spear the white flag's token.

Out of the battle we heard their trumpets answer,
scream like grey-eagles, arrogant and taunting,
sudden as that bright shaft the sun's gold lancer
laid in its rest against the morning, vaunting.
And courage, colder
Than our lost courage came as shoulder touched
with shoulder.

I chucked the pen down.

Shoulder to shoulder, I thought. The girls in the monkey parade. That was what the underlying restlessness was about. I muttered to myself: "I've had enough." To Flo, I said: "I think I'll go for a walk."

Outside, I told myself: What's the matter with me, I'm

an absolute ass. Writing stuff about courage and I haven't
a scrap. It's no way to find a girl, watching other chaps
getting 'em. I talked myself into courage and by the time
I reached the monkey parade, even boldness.

I saw three youths walking along and closed up behind
them, hoping the boys would not notice and the girls
think I was one of them. That strategy didn't work. On
my own again I tried different tactics. I altered my walk
to a swagger. I smiled at every girl who passed. I called
out, "Hello, there." I improved on that. I tried: "We've
met before haven't we?"

The girl gave a shriek. "Where? In La-di-Da Street?"

Girls, girls in their dozens went by. In their glancing
none sent me the signal for which my own glances
searched: an eye-flashing message 'I'd like to know you'.

I'd never find here a girl of my own kind. Why had I
joined the monkey parade? I shoved my hands into my
pockets, undecided what to do. I knew, but hazily, it
had been an idea – fed on hope – that *the* girl, wherever
she may be, would be directed by her own Kismet to
meet me tonight. Where *would* I find her? The girl I
thought Rose was to be, my own girl. For years, it
seemed to me I'd thought of no other girl but Rose.

Twilight was bringing out the lights of pubs. Girls
were pairing with the boys, and drifting towards East
End Park. I wasn't following them there tonight, I swung
the other way, towards town.

I saw myself imaged in the reflections of shop
windows, one in the crowd. I'd left the monkey parade,
lonely. I felt lonelier in this crowd. Families, going
home from the cinemas. People hurrying to catch late
tramcars. Old folk, slow moving. Late to bed kids,
running, weaving their way round people's legs. All going
somewhere, I thought. Most of them going home.

Love was there too. Separated from the crowd, making little havens for themselves in shop doorways, I saw the young lovers. Shy ones, standing close together, holding hands, pretending to be looking in the shop windows. Bolder ones, arms round each other talked and laughed. Then, in a darker doorway, a man with a girl in his arms bent her backwards, kissing her, kissing her. Her hair caught a glint, among the shadows, from a street lamp. Chestnut, chestnut, as Rose's had been . . . .

I had a stabbing sense of utter loss. I wandered on, there were fewer people about.

I stopped, not knowing whether to go on or to go back to Flo's.

A voice from a doorway called out; "Has yer girl gone home and left yer? Had a tiff?"

"I live just here, over the shop. Come with me, luv." She opened a door, I followed her up uncarpeted stairs, my heart hammering. A naked electric bulb was suddenly switched on. I was too confused to take in more than an impression of a frowsty room. She stripped off while I was getting out of my jacket.

"You've not been with a girl before, have you, dear?"

I hesitated, not wanting to say the betraying word, 'No'. I shook my head.

"There's always a first time, luv," she said. "Don't be shy. There's only me and you. Just leave it to me. I know just what to do."

She slid the braces over my shoulders.

"Never mind your shirt."

Skillful fingers nipped open my flies. As she touched my flesh an intrinsic part that had gone into the making of the I that was I, damped down. All the rest of my being centred in her hand.

It was soon over. She gave me a towel, showed me how

to use the permanganate. Disinfected? My whole being felt unclean. And I saw her. She had a wide lopsided mouth, mousy hair, matter-of-fact eyes. I looked at her, astounded that I had met her. Shamed at what I had done. The horrible, horrible, horrible thing was that what she had done to me and for me had been as impersonal as rain from an indifferent sky.

When she looked at me, her matter-of-fact eyes I saw were kindly. She said; "Never mind, dear, you'll do better next time. You know where to find me." I paid her more that she asked for, less than I owed, and stumbled down the stairs.

Flo was waiting up for me. Guilt, shame and the fact that I had known a woman must have been in my face for her to see.

What were these things to Flo, the pure in heart?

"There's a Cornish pasty waiting in the oven," she said.

Chapter 16

BIRD OF PARADISE

In the brick jungle the snow was black before it settled on the back-to-backs. "Have a good time, love," said Flo.. "We'll keep some mince pies for you when you come back home on New Year's eve."

Home? The word did not jar as it would have done a year before. In her own home, Flo had made a home for me.

Snow had not reached South Milford when Neville met me on the down platform.

"Merry Christmas, Ron. Ron, I came here straight from school. Except for a day at Grandma's of course. Ron, Tom's waiting with the car. Tom says Uncle Harold's thinking of buying a Beam in the new year. I'll carry the old case. We're going to have a turkey, a whopper."

Mr. Mook, the stationmaster, had added a festive sprig of mistletoe to his uniform lapel. He tore my ticket in half with a smiling, "Seasonable weather."

"Tom, where's Uncle?"

"Doing his rounds in the trap, Mr. Ronald."

Tom spoke approvingly. The Day-Leeds, that two-seater coupe with an engine as lovingly made as that of an early Rolls, had not yet seduced his heart from horses.

"If snow holds off — and I reckon it will — Doctor's set on going to the meet of the Badsworth at Darrington on Boxing Day. He'll be riding Snowball, with Judy as his second string."

"Can I come? And Ron, of course."

"Depends on what Doctor says."

"Aunt Ciss won't be going," said Neville gleefully.

"That's why Uncle is going to ride Snowball. Tom says the old boy can still take his fences like a three-year-old though he's . . . how old is Snowball, Tom?"

"Seventeen. And knows more about the Badsworth country than the huntsmen."

Neville jigged up and down.

"I want it to snow like billy-oh and I want to go to the meet on Boxing Day."

"You can't have both, master Neville, and that's a fact."

Winter dusk drew in early. Against it Ciss drew the brown velvet drapes in what was beginning to be called the lounge instead of the drawing-room. Harold didn't manage to take time off for afternoon tea, a break in a day liable to be unpredictably long-drawn out.

He was late for early dinner.

"It's too bad, Harold."

"Never mind, m'dear. With a bit of luck I can have my Christmas dinner in what passes on earth for peace. I'm snatching a quarter of an hour before the home surgery. I'll bring in some sand for planting the tree. Coming with me, Admiral?"

"You bet," I said.

"Me too," said Neville.

The roadmen had dumped cartloads of sand to deal with winter's anticipated ice.

There was one nearby.

When we piled out of the car the sand was already beginning to be sifted with an icing-sugar dredging of fine snow.

"Three buckets should do the trick."

We shovelled away till they were full.

Tom had set a wooden tub on layers of saved-up newspaper in the hall. Uncle and Tom half-filled the tub.

"Many waiting in the surgery, Tom?"

"No one with owt much wrong with 'em, Doctor. Or they'd have sent for you, if I know 'em. There's old Mrs Jackson."

"I told her to stay in bed. Ah, well." Harold went off down the passage to the back door. Heaps of holly in the passage, with berries as vivid as sealing-wax scarlet.

My cousin Joan, fair, eleven and fizzing with excitement, sat on the stairs pulling out paper-chains and opening Christmas bells. Leaning over the banisters to toss the decorations over for me to hang up, she chattered non-stop and I scarcely listened. I knotted whipcord to the tails of Christmas Past to criss-cross holly, tinsel, paper-chains and soundless bells above the trees the rest were dressing.

Harold came back and lifted Joan to switch on the fairy lights the indefatigable Tom had wired.

"I've just prescribed myself Captain Hook's bicarbonate of soda," he said, "I'd mortally offend the wives of all my patients if I refused their slices of plumcake, wedges of Wensleydale and mince pies."

He turned out his side pockets into an upturned hunting bowler.

"Can I have a piece, Daddy?" said Joan. "The marzipan looks scrumptious."

"Just one, to be taken before bedtime. Doctor's orders."

At eleven the carollers brought in an icy draught flecked with snow, and a Chinese lantern as warmly aglow as their faces.

"Once in royal Daa-avid's city . . . . " Handbells counterpointed the youthful voices.

With a thrill of shock I heard my father's voice singing from among the group.

"Joyful and triumphant . . . " I listened, yearning . . . The voice was that of my brother Neville — he had the same light baritone. I turned aside my head.

"I've kept your mince pies," said Flo.

"I like yours better than South Milford's," I told her.

"Give over."

"I mean it."

I did, too. Flo kept on looking at me. I wondered if she had intuitively understood the sense in which I'd used the word 'like'. Because Flo, who had so little, had out of the goodness of her heart taken the trouble to lay them on one side for me. I knew by now that she could read in my eyes thoughts I sometimes didn't apprehend myself at the back of my mind.

She said, "Did you meet any nice girls, love?"

So that was what she'd read at the back of my mind. "Cynthia."

"Is she very pretty?"

Was she? "I don't know. She'd been away from Milford for a few years. I remembered her as a leggy schoolgirl. My cousin Joan, well, she's eleven now, she's always had parties in the rectory Sunday school. It used to be blind man's buff and pinning the tail on the donkey. Kids' games. Now it's dances. With Cynthia it's like dancing with about two ounces of thistledown."

"You've fallen in love with her."

"All the poets have fallen in love with Cynthia. One of them, Milton, named her.

Where Cynthia checks her dragon yoke
nightly o'er the accustomed oak.

"Yeats called her:

. . . a glimmering girl
with apple blossom in her hair
who called me by my name and ran
and faded on the brightening air . . . "

"You *are* in love?" Flo laughed. She was used to my spouting poetry.

"I think she was Shakespeare's Rosalind. In the forest of Arden. You know . . . " I had just made the discovery. "He described his girls in his sonnets.

Shall I compare thee to a summer's day?
Thou art more lovely and more temperate . . .

"He showed them to us in his plays. If wireless and the cinema had been invented in his day, Shakespeare would have made pots of money. Great sweeping panoramic stuff. He'd have used wireless I think, for the plays he put his heart into.

"Falstaff telling rumbustious great lies about the men in buckram. Romeo making love to Juliet. Mad, blind old Lear carrying in his arms Cordelia, dead. I think, one day, the cinema may become a great art form. It will never outsoar the newest art form of them all. Wireless.

"Who wants to know that the battlements of Elsinore looked like a Swedish match factory? Shakespeare, who put an ass's head on Bottom the Weaver, would have used wireless to transplant men's eyes and ears.

190

Look, Jessica, see where the floor of heaven is thick inlaid with patines of bright gold."

I was talking to myself, and Flo, knowing it, let me have my head. But she listened and brought back my spouting to the subject that really interested her.

"Do you talk to Cynthia like this?"

"I will, if I get half a chance."

I looked at my hands on the gaslit tablecloth overlaid with green crepe paper. I had managed to scrape the dirt of the machine shop with a nail file. Neither soap and hot water nor pumice stone had wholly cleansed my skin of the sump oil I so loathed.

"Fat lot of use my thinking about Cynthia. If my uncle James hadn't put his foot down and stopped me going to Oxford when I was eighteen . . . . Oh, Flo, I'd have taken my finals last June. Know what James did do? Before he chucked me into the machine shop he got me an interview with the editor of the *Yorkshire Post*. Chap called Osborn. A mason. Trust James for that. Osborn told him that being deaf, I'd never make a journalist. Which clinched James' own opinion. Joke is, Osborn was no more a journalist than James himself. He's the joint general manager. A business man. To be fair to James he probably thought Osborn *was* the editor. Tell you another thing. First year I was at Scriven's I saved money. As you know, my wages were not stopped during the general strike. Thanks to my guardian angel my shirts were laundered, my overalls washed, my socks darned, my buttons sewn on."

"Give over, love. Ee, as my Herbert said, you were the only breadwinner."

I shook my head. "Maybe, Flo, but in all honesty I tell you, I've never done one honest day's work for my pay."

191

Why should I care? As long as James shook his head
I was unsackable. Sighted, in Gaza, at the mill with
slaves, I let the lathe saddle make traverse after traverse
without shaving any metal off at all. All round me
highly skilled, bloodily badly paid men were making
what to some of them were poems in steel. There were
times even in the midst of the machines' inferno of
sound when in my head Kit Marlowe's voice sang of the
face that launched a thousand ships and burned the
topless towers of Ilium. I listened to Sir Thomas Browne
wondering what song the sirens sang — until the
machine shop siren, screaming like Medusa, set me free.

So the days of summer trudged on and after the siren
sang, took wing. The evenings flew the faster when I
went to Denis Botterill's flat in Woodhouse Square.

I'd met Denis in the best secondhand bookshop in
town. The tupenny dip box had lured me inside. About
my third visit a fair-haired young fellow with a cleft in
his chin said: "You like poetry, don't you? So do I. I
write a bit. Care to have a bit of a natter with me when
the shutters go up? My name's Botterill. I work here."

I joined him in the Cobourg. A Victorian pub in the
hinterland of the university's Latin quarter. I'd no
intention of having a drink and our friendship nearly
ended before it had started when Denis discovered I
meant my refusal. The meeting sparked off a poem I was
to write later.

Mind with mind can meet and match
essence, death and quality,
at a glance accept, refuse,
bolt the door or lift the latch . . .

Denis tried persuasion, mockery and downright rudeness.
But I was as stubbornly Yorkshire as Denis. Afterwards
I helled around with Denis and his friends. They drank.

I sipped about two fingers of Schweppes orange cordial topped up with ice-cream soda.

"The rake's progress," said Denis.

"He'll be graduating to sarsparilla next week." They were good chaps and soon tired of nagging me.

In Denis' flat I couldn't keep away from his bookshelves. He had a penchant for the Americans. 'The Love Song of J. Alfred Prufrock'.

Apeneck Sweeney among his nightingales. Leaves of grass. And the early Vachell Lindsay enchanted us with his liveliness.

We chorused:

"Fat black bucks in a wine-barrel room,
barrelhouse kings with feet unstable
sagged and reeled and pounded on the table,
pounded on the table . . . "

We pounded away like Wellington at Waterloo. "Hi," yelled Denis, "Not with Untermeyer, it's a first edition."

We chanted back at him.

"With a silk umbrella and the handle of a broom,
hard as they were able,
BOOM BOOM BOOM."

I went for his poets, then for the prose.

Melomaniacs by James Huneker. Joseph Hergesheimer's *Java Head*. Carl van Vechten's *Firecrackers*. Frank Norris's *The Pit*. F. Scott Fitzgerald's *The Beautiful and the Damned* on top of this went to my head more than the jam-jars of beer and the bottles of wine went to the heads of the others. Joseph Moncure March's *The Wild Party* set us a mark to aim at. We wore out boxes of gramophone needles on Irving Berlin and Schubert, Chopin.

"YES, WE HAVE NO BANANAS, WHEN IT'S MIDNIGHT IN ITALY."

People swarmed up from the flat below to lynch us when we rolled back the carpet and Charlestoned until books fell out of the bookcases.

"Denis, Denis, Denis," laughed Flo. "You never have time to talk to me these days . . . Have all those wonderful girls with Eton crops and jade cigarette holders made you forget Cynthia, too?"

"No."

"What does Denis say about her?"

"I've never mentioned her to Denis."

"But you show him the poems you write, don't you, love?"

"Sometimes.His are so much better."

"I like the poems you write. I never used to read poetry at all after I left school. Yet I can remember most of what we did learn.

Drake he's in his hammock an' a thousand mile away,

(Capten, art tha sleepin' there below?) . . .

And

The Gatling's jammed and the Colonel dead,

And the regiment blind with dust and smoke . . .

"I didn't know what a gatling was and I don't know now. But that was one of my favourite bits . . . You talking about poetry made me take an interest again. Where we live isn't the sort of place you could write poetry about, is it?"

"I'll write a poem about you, Flo."

"Give over. I'm not worth writing a poem about."

I cleared my quarter-deck and took a writing tablet from behind the tin alarm clock. I began:

"Her mean drab cage of brick and stone,

the grim North country's sullen own,

Flo's mind makes an aviary

where birds of brilliant plumage fly a place aloud with
chirrupings with starts and flickers of bright wings,
wherein all day she trills and sings.
The milkman calls and leaves two gills.
At once the tale her quick tongue spills of how he
told her, for a fact,
that Jem, next door but four, is sacked.
And her expecting!
Tragedy!
Flo's thoughts, from this calamity dip, swerve and
twist — they fly to all friends ever ill in hospital,
with sudden dartings and escapes
to flowers and the price of grapes.
From which, in turn, they glance aside to
childhood treats at Whitsuntide,
skimming across these common things
with oh, such eager flutterings
nectar sips, ideas and words
blur like the wings of humming birds.
Each hideous China ornament she dusts — each
brilliant argument with
the Gasman or the Rates. The grocery bills,
street hawkers' cries,
these things upon her tongue she tries all day.
The enchanting song she pours, soon as her Herbert
comes indoors.
He answers "aye" or "nay" and is content, his duty
said, to eat his fill and shake his head —
two cups for Flo, one slice of bread.
He takes scant notice, he is wise. for Flo on
honeydew has fed, being a bird of paradise."
"That's very nice. It's lovely," said Flo.
She gave a little flick of her apron at me.
"Go on with you, calling me a bird of paradise."

195

"But that's exactly what you are."

She sat down.

"I think I'll have another cuppa. I'm not like that, really. Not inside. I like looking after Herbert and you. You laugh at me for washing my bits of ornaments. Herbert scolds me for scrubbing the brickwork and donkey-stoning the kerb but what would he say if I didn't and Number Three were the only house that let Sebastopol Street down?"

"And the only Mrs Mester doesn't "borrow" a twist of tea or a shovel of coal from? The only one little Annie never pops in to? I know."

"Mrs Mester has a hard life," Flo reproached. "You don't know, Ron. Oh, dear." She made her familiar gesture of tidying her hair at the temple with the back of her hand.

"You've made me forget. This came for you by the late afternoon post."

The South Milford postmark.

"Aunt Ciss wants me to go over for the weekend," I told Flo. "H'mm. I *was* thinking of going to Ilkley with Denis."

"Denis, Denis, Denis." Flo laughed.

"You give him back word, and go and see your Auntie."

Flo came to the door to see me off.

"Good night," she said, "God bless."

It was just short of midnight on Sunday when I got back to Sebastopol Street. Light, shrouded by Flo's lace curtains gleamed through the window of Number Three. Flo, of course, was sitting up for me. I opened the door. The room was stuffed with people. Some sort of a party? Mrs. Mester. Little Annie, the popper-ins. Friends and neighbours from the Inkermans, the Balaclavas. They all gawped at me. I said: "What's up with you all? You look as though you've just come back from a funeral."

There was a dreadful silence. Mrs Mester blurted: "It's Flo. She died at five past four this morning."

Then someone moved and I saw Herbert. He was slumped in his chair like an ox which has been poleaxed.

Night has let fall over the Balaclavas, the Inkermans, the Sebastopols a pall woven of the wasted, the lost, the broken, the bitter bloody years over the grey, the hopeless, the indomitable men of the brickwork jumble of the back-to-backs, the engineers who made the machines which make the machines, the billet-breakers, the plate-edge planers, the lathes, the borers: the machines which built the bridges of Dorman, Longs, the Titanic, the Mauretania, the splendid ships launched from the slips of Tyne and Tees and Clyde to ride the waves of the five oceans, the seven seas. The men who made the machines which make the machines their slaves in wage-chains, cloth caps and foul blue jeans starved and cast aside, thrown on the scrap heap like their labour, their rusted tools.

As Masefield cried: "The men hemmed in by the spears."

As Shakespeare said with laughter through his tears:

"And all our yesterdays have lighted fools the way to dusty death."

I will remember them. While I draw breath I will not forget them, the grey men broken as steel was broken by their billet-breakers. I will remember them as I remember the poets, the music makers. Whatever strain and stress I undergo this side of that undiscovered country from whose bourne no traveller returns, I will remember Flo, the pure in heart, the only purity. I will remember the last words she ever spoke to me: "Goodnight. God bless."

Chapter 17

THE WASTELAND

The Dead — says the Spanish proverb — to their graves.
The living to their dinners.

But dinners must be earned. Life goes on. After Flo's
funeral I went on to my grandmother's in Ellers Road.
In her own sweet way, she comforted me.

Herbert, a broken man, was back at his vertical
milling-machine less than a week later. He'd nothing to
say when I went across to him. What could he have said?
I learned roundabout that neighbours had rallied round.
They, who lived from hand to mouth themselves, understood with no words spoken, how to cope. Somebody
cooked his breakfast. There was a meal waiting for him
when he went home. Little Annie, the popper in, popped
in. Herbert, the steady breadwinner, scarcely knew the
price of a loaf of bread. Bread continued to find its way
into the crock.

I felt lost and desolate. What must Herbert have felt?
The wordless answer was the man himself.

A fortnight later, as the works siren was wailing down
the scale in the sudden, shocked quietness of the works,

198

I was washing my arms in sump oil when Herbert came across.

"If you want to come back, lad, you can. I've got a woman to come and do for me."

We bought fish-and-chips on the way home. Home? As we turned the corner into Sebastopol Street with never another word spoken, desolation overcame me. Again I had no home. Herbert opened the door.

"Oh," said the woman who was sitting at the table.

"I didn't know you was bringing *him* back today I'd best see . . . " She wrinkled her nose.

"You've got fish-n'-chips eh? I'll set another place."

As she departed she said over her shoulder: "Mrs Mays'll be doing your breakfasts."

Flo was everywhere in her empty birdcage.

Its silence was filled by the trills of her tongue. Her wings fluttered from branch to branch of the day's dramatic, raptly inconsequential events. Nothing seemed changed, except Herbert, the background of her neverending song. The tablecloth was clean. Some woman had washed it. The small range had been blackleaded. But soon dust filmed the Gosse china ornaments. The silver frame of her wedding photo had not been polished.

And Herbert said nothing and I said nothing, until I smelled fumes coming from the oven.

"There's something burning," I jumped up.

Whatever it had been the woman had put in and forgotten was unrecognisably charred.

I took it on the pavement to cool. The brickwork, up to the bedroom windowsill, that Flo had kept scrubbed clean was beginning to grime again.

As I straightened, I knew that eyes were watching me. The curtains of Number Six had three holes in them — Flo and I used to laugh — two for Mrs Walker's eyes, one for her nose. She and Mrs Mester were the only two in Sebastopol Street who had not gone over to do whatever they could for Herbert.

I went back. The washing up had been simple. I'd burnt the newspaper wrappings of our fish and chips. What to do? I began to slide the teapot, pint mugs and sugar bowl from my end of the table. I'd write a poem. But what about? I hadn't felt like writing since Flo died. I looked at Herbert. I said: "I'm going to my grand-mother's to fetch a few of my things."

"Aye," said Herbert.

I realised, abruptly, that like him I was still in my mechanic's overalls.

After a good hot bath, I told my grandmother: "I'm going back to Sebastopol Street. I've got to live near the works."

When I got back to Sebastopol Street, there was no light in the living room. Herbert had gone to bed. Half way up the stairs in the dark, my head began to throb. The swinging arc lamp on its cross wires dipped its wing of darkness as I opened the door. One step, and the arc lamp swung up its glaring sweep of light. Somebody had made my bed. As I undressed the throbbing in my head shifted from my temples to the back of my neck. I heard sounds that were not in my room — THUT THUT THUTTER — but in the works. THUT, thut, thut. The sounds were in my head. I flung myself on the bed. In about ten minutes the throbbing had gone. Then I slept.

At the works next morning as soon as the gas engine started up the throbbing came back. Over the years, I had gradually become used to the din. Its overall clamour seemed to cancel the individual shrieks and screams. The monotonous beat of the great gas engine had a basic rhythm to which my ear had become accustomed. This tolerance was being broken down. Now the voices of the different machines yelled into my throbbing head. As they had done in my first day in the machine-shop.

I was in bedlam again. In a bedlam of voices. Words stuttered into my brain. Frighteningly unrhythmic words. THUTTER, went the gas engine. No hope. Highspeed electric drills bit into me, screaming. No way 'out.

As the morning wore on, my ear became tolerant of the clamour again. Bedlam became its normal background clamour.

When Herbert and I got back to the house the woman had our meal ready. The tea was black-strong and she had sweetened it with condensed milk, I couldn't drink it. Being hungry I ate the limp, boiled-in-water kippers. She'd made a bread and butter pudding with maggyann and soused it with something out of a tin. I ate next to nothing.

One day, THUT, the rhythm of the gas engine seemed to have changed. THUTTER. It no longer beat in my head. A changed rhythm. I knew some kind of change was taking place in myself which I'd got to think about. Changes took place in the house while Herbert and I were at work. Changes, which on our return, Herbert never seemed to notice. Pieces of furniture had been moved from Flo's happy placing and set down where the woman wanted them. Flo's wedding photograph had disappeared. One evening, after she'd washed up, the woman said:

"I've brought a set of doms. Let's have a game, eh?"

Her conversation had an appalling, flat triviality all the deadlier because her voice had a penetrating quality I could hear only too well. Playing dominoes, she became shrill.

"Always keep a two-a-two."

She rapped a domino on the table.

"I'm out."

She pushed the dominoes over to Herbert.

"Your shuffle, Bert." She gave Herbert a familiar nudge. I felt as affronted as though she had nudged me.

Putting on her coat ready to go she said: "I may as well leave my apron — I'll be back first thing in the morning."

At the door she said: "It's been a very pleasant evening, Bert. We must have some more."

I knew I couldn't stand another evening like it. I didn't have to. Next evening she said: "I bet I could beat you in a two-hander, Bert."

Herbert grunted: "That you can't."

The woman slapped the box on the table and spread the dominoes.

"It's a challenge," she said. "Pick a dom, Bert. Highest goes first."

I felt stifled. I couldn't go out. I took my notepaper up to my room. I couldn't write a line. I brooded over the increasing frightfulness of my world. There was no way out. No hope. "Get out," a voice inside me said. "Get out now."

Hope? It was the height of the depression which had America by the throat. Men were jumping out of the windows of skyscrapers, putting pistols to their heads, cutting their throats. The repercussions of that cataclysm were sending seismic tremors throughout the Western world. Great firms, household names in textiles, shipping, engineering, were crashing in England. Scrivens was standing the hammer but I knew they had not declared a dividend for years. Get out? No hope. As long as I was protected by Uncle James I had a job. And what had I been doing, shielded by him? Wasting my time, eating my heart out in a job which should have been done by any one of a couple of hundred mechanics far more competent than I was and with bread to win for their own, and here was I making wasters of every repetition job I did. Keeping decent chaps, skilled workmen out in the streets, propping up walls, idling, vacant-eyed, at street corners. Any one of them would have thanked God to have been in my shoes.

THUTTER. THUT. My head started throbbing again. I dreaded increasingly the clamour voices of the machines.

One day was like another: hell. One night was like another: hell. But it seemed to me that I was wandering through different circles of the same hell, seeking a way out.

I could have spent a week-end at South Milford. THUT. No. No hope. I sent my distracted mind there. Contaminate what was the greenest of my cages with the hell I knew I would take with me if I went? THUTTER.

But one week-end I went to my grandmother's in Ellers Road. In her clean, little house I smelt my own uncleanliness. I soaked and soaked in the hottest water I could bear and used loofah, sponge, soap and pumice stone.

I had a frightful end-of-the-tether desperation. I had to talk to *somebody*. To Denis Botterill. I knew where to find Denis. He was working in Miles's bookshop in Queen's Square. He kept longer hours than I had to. He was just about to leave when I walked into the shop.

"Good to see you," Denis said. He put his coat on. "Good God, man, you look hellish rough." He gave me a clout on the shoulder. "Come along to the Cobourg, sink your tom-fool ideas about strong drink raging, and sink a pint." We went to the Cobourg.

I said, "I'll buy you a pint, Denis, lemonade, as per, for me."

"What's up with you man? You'll never write poetry on lemonade."

I told him: "I can't write poetry any more. I know I never will."

Denis sank his pint.

"Spit it out," he said.

I spat it out. The lot. Denis looked at me as I spoke. He listened to my outpourings.

"Ronald, you're a sick man," he said. "What about that relative of yours in South Milford. Doctor, isn't he? Better see him."

I knew he was right, I said, "I know, I *do* know. I might even do as you say, Denis. But right now, you're the only doctor I need."

I went back to Sebastopol Street late. The woman had left the gas light on, very low. She'd pushed the sofa back against the wall. She was asleep on it. Flo's alarm clock was on the floor beside her.

When I got into bed I knew at once that the sheets and the pillow case had been changed. The sheets were coarse and smelled of cheap soap. The pillow case was threadbare. Bitch. Bitch. Bitch.

Resenting so strongly the presence of this woman in the house that was still, to me, Flo's house, I tried to argue myself out of idealism into reality. What concern was it of mine? Yet I had a confused notion that I was being loyal to Flo. Her 'Bird of Paradise' presence was with me always through whatever turmoil my own spirit was enduring.

How many days or weeks it was I cannot now recall. I remember the night the sofa was no longer pushed against the wall. The woman wasn't there. Flo's clock was not on the mantlepiece.

Rage kept me awake. Where is the borderline between sleeping and waking? I crossed it by the bridge of emotional exhaustion.

The disintegration was gradual. It seemed to me that first one machine would have a go at me, then another. I wandered about within myself through a confused and confusing maze.

I reset the traversing saddle of my lathe, not bothering to adjust the cutting tool to shave off the next steel paring. I watched the saddle moving. I was supposed to turn out a worm-gear for the self-stoking furnaces every twenty minutes.

My head was splitting apart.

At the end of the traverse I stopped the lathe and took out the cutting tool. I went to the tool-fitter's store to swap the cutter for a new one. It was quite a walk. I took my time. Clangour followed me. No way out.

Returning to my machine, Bob Fieldhouse was waiting for me, watch in hand. "Tha's been away sixteen minutes wi' thi' lathe doin' nowt. An' look at them bloody wasters. There's more on t' floor there than wor scrapped t' first day tha started. What's up wi' thi'? Call thissen a Scriven? Thi' dad would 'ave 'ad summat to say to thee. By gow."

"Damn your impudence. If my father were alive I wouldn't bloody well be here. Neither would you. Foreman? You aren't fit to sweep the sodding floors."

His face flushed a dull red. He started to move away. I hadn't finished with Bob Fieldhouse.

"Hold on," I said, "You call me deaf and daft. Next time you think of describing me to your mates — try applying some of your own preaching on accuracy."

"Cheeky bastard," Bob took himself over to the planer.

He stood watching me. Bloody-minded bastard yourself. I stared back at him. I wouldn't start the lathe till he shifted. My own machine still, made the others more penetrating. They roared at me: Not fit, not fit. Scriven, they thutted at me my grandfather's name. Scriven, Scriven, they beat at me my father's name. Scriven, Scriven, Scriven they pounded at me my own name. Scrivens, they screeched at me the name of the firm. Sod Scrivens. Bob Fieldhouse, I saw, had gone. I pulled the lever. I flung at the machine every filthy word I knew. I let it run on its own. I kicked at the wasted stuff knowing I'd been wasting more and more material these past months. I didn't bloody care. I would be meeting Denis tonight in the Cobourg. Get the bedlam day over.

As my life was shifted from the machine shop to Sebastopol Street, from Sebastopol Street to the machine shop, I was all the time seeking a way to get myself back on to an even keel . . . some way . . . Then, it came into my head that I could beat the pandemonium if I could shut out all its voices except one. I'd listen to the scream of my lathe and master that voice. How? My mind was logical, wasn't it? I would master the machine by mastering the lathe itself. I would master its voice by my own voice.

I started the rough cut. Concentrated on the cutting edge biting into the black, sandblistered steel. "Now, you spiralling, red-hot serpent, scream." The serpent screamed. "Now for the second, and finer cut. There, you see. Going quite smoothly. The third must be the finishing cut and smooth, accurate to a fiftieth, smooth mirror smooth."

A tickling chuckled into my throat, I was laughing.

I adjusted the machine. "Bite, you bugger, bite." The cutting edge bit. It had bitten far too deeply and I had ruined yet one more worm gear. Instantly, all the voices of bedlam were at me again. I tried to shut out the monstrous cacophony from my ears by staring at the driving belt. From the overhead shafting the great belt which drove all the machines revolved round the gas engine's great flywheel. Round and round . . . no beginning . . . no ending. Only stopping. Stopping? Was that the way out for me? No THUT, THUTTER shattered the thoughts that revolved round and round in my head. No screech of the planer drove them out.

Suicide? The Naysmith hammer's pound — was it yes? was it no?

I do not remember how many days I lived through nor how many ways to commit suicide I considered and rejected. One night in my room which, by its size and shape and the state of my mind appeared to me to be coffin-like, I found my answer. Poison. I knew where Uncle Harold kept the spare key of his Poison cupboard. I'd only to go to South Milford and get the stuff. Poison would do the trick quickly. Where to take it? Swim out into the Wharfe and take it there? I'd already discarded the idea of drowning myself. On the moors? Somewhere deep in the bracken, if left long enough, I'd be unrecognisable when found. The tickling chuckling in my throat started me laughing, I laughed at myself for laughing, I couldn't stop. No, I'd take the poison here, in this room, on this bed that was already like a coffin. I laughed out loud. I'd black my face and when the woman found me she'd die of fright. It was so good, I went to the Cobourg to tell Denis. Denis was with a group of friends. He lifted his glass when he saw me and called out, "We're breaking up in a few minutes, Ron, hang on." I bought myself a lemonade and 'hung on'. Denis joined me. He lent me his ear.

I didn't know what I'd expected from him when I'd finished, I only knew he was right when he said, "Out, out brief candle? Not you."

"Why not?" I said. "Chatterton did. He was a poet. The marvellous boy, he snuffed his brief candle at nineteen."

Denis laughed, "You need cutting down to size. You're no marvellous boy."

"Good lord, Denis, I didn't mean it that way. You know damn well I didn't." I felt angry. Denis didn't let up on me. "Don't talk any more tosh about poetry being hammered out of you. You're bloody well living the stuff of the poetry you're going to write. I'm a bit of a poet, Ron. I know. Christ, the way you've been talking about those damned machines, you had them pounding in *my* head." Denis finished his pint. He said, "Now, come on round to the flat. The people you saw me with will be dropping in." He looked at his watch. "They'll be there now."

At Denis' flat there were some of his friends and some of their friends. We opened bottles. We played records, we fox-trotted. We tried to Charleston in the too-small room. We laughed as we kicked one another. I sweated oil and I didn't care and they didn't care. We ate fish-and-chips out of their paper wrappings. We all talked at once, and we all talked to each other. We pulled governments down. We set the world to rights.

Back in Sebastopol Street I slept as I'd never slept. I could have slept for a week if Herbert hadn't banged on the door.

As I was punching the time machine, Bob Fieldhouse, the foreman said, "Mr. James wants to see you."

Defiance, speeding my way to his office, set my brain at greater speed on what I would say to him when the attack came.

Uncle was seated at his desk. James looked like a man with a lot on his mind, I felt no pity. I said, "I know why you've sent for me, Uncle. Fieldhouse has told you about my botching the job."

Uncle James considered this before he spoke:

"That, among other things, Ronald."

"Then let's have the other things, as I know all about . . . "

James started to smoulder.

"You know, you know, you tomfool, you know nothing. And don't stand over me in that manner. Sit down. I'm going to say what I have to say. Do you think this is the first I've heard about your atrocious work? Do you not feel shame that at a time like this when every ounce of material should be used, not wasted . . . with the country in the state its in . . . "

I sat down.

"Uncle, you've no need to go any further. There's nothing you are saying that I haven't felt. I'm sickened and more than sickened for my own reasons as well as yours."

He sensed my truth and was perplexed.

"Then why, in heaven's name have you not applied yourself to learning? Your grandfather, your father, myself, none of us could have done what we have done unless we had started on the shop floor. I would have arranged long ago to move you up the ladder . . . "

"I'm sorry. Uncle, it's no use."

"What's the matter with you? Have you no pride? Why, the name of Scriven is on machinery in Naval Bases all over the world."

"Pride? of course I've pride. I'm a Scriven. But not an engineer. I never will be. Uncle, can't you see my point of view? I want to prove *myself*. My grandfather proved *himself*. His name is on machinery. I want to see R.C. Scriven at the end of a poem. In print."

"Let us not resume that subject here. I had thought that such nonsense would have been cleared out of your head when you discovered that there was no means of earning a living by writing." He stood up. "More to the point, is what you are doing with the wages you take out of the firm. I have heard that you are seen frequenting the Cobourg. A public house full of riff-raff, ne'er-do-wells and prostitutes. Apparently you can think of no way to use your wages to better purpose than chucking it away on drink."

I jumped to my feet, my face close to his. Heat from our bodies filled the space between us. Heat from our tempers slashed our minds wholly apart.

"I don't drink."

James snorted.

"I tell you again, *I don't drink*."

James shouted; "It's enough that you are seen in low public houses, associating with the scum of Leeds."

"You may thank your informants for me, Uncle. Tell them to look out for me tonight." James crashed his fist on the desk.

"Insolence." He sat down. "This is the last straw, Ronald. There is no more I am prepared to do for you. I shall arrange for our cashier to prepare your cards for this Saturday."

On Saturday I collected my pay packet. I was handed *two* envelopes. One contained my wages, 25/- plus my holiday pay, the other a £10 note and a letter from uncle.

Dear Ronald, Your Aunt Florence is very grieved by what I have told her. We both wish you to know that you are still welcome to visit us at Moorlands. Here enclosed, is ten pounds from us both. Affectionately yours, Uncle James.

Good lord, I was certain that I'd been cast out in a never-darken-my-door-again style by James. I read his letter again and was glad. Ten quid? With the twenty-odd pounds I'd saved over the years from my family's birthday and Christmas gifts, I was rich.

In the basement stove of Denis's flat we ceremoniously burnt my foul blue overalls. Denis said. "A burnt offering to the gods, Ron?"

"A sacrifice to whatever gods may be." I said.

I went back to Ellers Road. Of course my grandmother had heard what had happened. "Now you can make a fresh start," she said. She gave me the attic room Neville and I had shared in the school hols. I tried to write. I couldn't. Headaches came. They went. Noises, traffic sounds set my head throbbing. In about three weeks they had gone. Grandma and the peace in her little box of bricks had restored me.

One evening after tea I felt conflicting impulses. The day had been overcast, then drizzly. Physical, barometric pressure made me restive. A different restlessness reacted inside me. I put on my raincoat. For a moment I was undecided. Then I set off. I walked to the tram stop, I knew where I was going.

I had come to a high place as is the instinct of a man to do when he wants to be alone. I spread my mac on the grass, now nearly dry, put my hands behind my head, looked up at the stars and let the wind blow over me.

Behind and below me was the glow of the lights of Leeds. Above, no moon in a rain-washed sky, the planet of evening, leading out her train of attendant stars. Lying there, I tried not to think at all. I would empty my mind of everything that had happened to me. The wind was fresh and I breathed it in deeply. I would fill the whole of my being with the almost-nothingness of air. Nothing. Nothing. Nothing.

My blood began to beat. My heart-rhythm pulsed wordlessly in my head. A kind of humming. Then, as September swallows alight on a telephone line, words, words came and settled on the rhythm-line. Random words, from nowhere. Silver. Trees. Sandal. Another word flew into my head uninvited. Tangled. Throw thoughts, words out of my head while I was conscious? I might as well try to empty the sky of stars and fling the froth of the Milky Way over the five continents and the seven seas. Seas . . . Seas . . . Trees . . . and suddenly the random words which had alighted on the heart-rhythm in my head sang out.

'And silver-sandalled Hesperus tangled in the summer trees.'

Overpowering excitement sent the words flying. The power of making poetry had returned to me. Not the power. The gift. A gift which it is death to throw away. The power, ah, that was very different. Only the very great ones had that. The power to relate any one thing in the universe to any other. I'd never have that. But the gift was mine. The shining gift which is lavished on children and artists who are little more than children grown up.

The gift which enables a child to see gold in a rain-puddle. An artist knows that rain-gold is only called fool's gold by fools.

A gift greater than perennial youth, because with it man keeps to the end of his days wonder, marvel and delight.

This gift had been given to me and I had dared

contemplate returning it to the giver, its brightness disfigured by death's cancellation stamp.

For a moment I stayed image-still. I wanted to experience to the full the wonderful feeling that my body and my mind were at one again. Whole, lucid, illumined, as a lamp is by the flame of the spirit within.

I was free. What lay ahead? The future. What had I got, I asked myself, with which to face the future? The goodwill of my family. A few pounds and the gift of poetry. What, I asked myself had I to overcome? Deafness? What was deafness but to be overcome? I had already come a long way – and gained – in my attempts to overcome my deafness.

Fear? I knew myself to be free at last from fear of my own incompetence. I stood up.

To the south-east, softened by distance, I saw a stronger glow where the tilted cone of a blast-furnace glared redly, like Algol, the Demon's eye, remoter than Mars.

In the night even eyesores of the industrial revolution were magicked in beauty. And beauty was in them by day for eyes which could really see.

An older word for poet than 'maker', a stronger word is 'seer'. While I had the use of my eyes I would use them for their god-given purpose. Whatever I looked at, I promised myself, would stay looked at as long as I drew breath. I looked into the light-bowl, the night-bowl of my father's city. In its mysterious interplay of light and shadow lay the future. My future among others.

I went down from my high place to meet the future. I went to meet it with hope and confidence, knowing that whatever it held in store, was to become an integral part of me.

Chapter 18

A BLIND UNDERSTANDING

Most of us have seen at one time or another, a complete circular rainbow haloing the sun or the moon. Its appearance, caused by atmospheric condition, is a foul-weather portent.

When I first began to see this faint, lovely, dangerous thing in fair weather conditions I put it down to eye strain.

Floating in the sea off the hollow land of Holderness when I was sixteen, I'd taken the halo, when it appeared round the sun, to be just such a weather sign. The beautiful rings, red, orange, yellow, green, blue, indigo, violet had faded in a few minutes.

It was years before I noticed them again, circling the moon. This halo, too, faded but not quickly.

The next time, I saw other haloes in broad daylight, wavering, beautiful round every point of light: a struck match, a window catching a flash of the sun itself.

Eyestrain.

Natural phenomena, I told myself. Like the dull lovely rainbows of rain puddles scummed by petrol.

214

These took their time in fading but never lasted overnight. Eyestrain. I was a prodigious reader.

I began to suspect something of the truth when in my late teens a night's sleep failed to banish the illusion. I let long intervals, of months, and sometimes of a whole year, between the illusions lull me into thinking there was nothing much wrong with my eyes. I wanted to be lulled. Deep in my mind I was afraid. I paid a great price for my cowardice.

A price I paid very slowly. Between the land of the sighted and the country of the blind lies a frontier. Sometimes that frontier is crossed with frightful suddenness. A car crash, a spark which sets off an explosion in the pit-damp in the gallery of a mine, a shot-gun carelessly handled: and one is blind for life. Glaucoma, neglected for whatever reason, acts very slowly. It took me many years to cross the shadowy borderland at the end of which I knew too late I must grope my way as best I could in stone blindness.

But one learns philosophy on long journeys or not at all. Long before I took the last stage of my journey towards darkness, I knew my real journey was towards "that undiscovered country from whose bourne no traveller returns."

I did not journey alone into the shadows. Before I knew I had to undertake it I had chosen good companions, the poets. Early on Hilaire Belloc had given me sound advice.

From quiet homes and first beginning
out to the undiscovered ends
there's nothing worth the wear of winning
but laughter and the love of friends.

I've always been rich in friends. Over the years, the deeper the shadows became the closer my invisible companions gathered around me, to them, my own kind, the poets, the makers, deafness was no barrier.

"The mind," Milton told me, "is its own place, and of itself can make a hell of heaven, a heaven of hell."

What they told me refreshed my spirit, sustained me in the more arduous and arid stretches of the wasteland through which, to my mind, the greatest of them in this century, T. S. Eliot, made his way.

Of course I stumbled, of course I sometimes fell and bruised myself, physically. Of course I lashed out and hurt those who loved me. Of course I resented losing among the shadows trees, birds, flowers, animals, the round globe itself. Of course I let go of my sense of proportion so that pinpricks hurt me more than thorns did. Pinpricks. Well-meaning folk, strangers would say I was making a good go of it − and I would say in my head: Yes, have a go yourself at being blind. And afterwards despise myself for such a cheap and childish self-outburst. I, who had told myself: There are only two things a man can do about a grievous disability. Put up with it, or fold up. Of course. Of course. But Housman said to me:

I won it in a weary land,
wrung from a stem that scored the hand.
But take it. If the brew be sour, the better
for the embittered hour.

And the laughing ones, the light verse poets, Tom Hood for one, would say:

The parson told the sexton
and the sexton tolled the bell.

My journey through the wasteland with such companions made me, above all, one of their company. I'd written my first radio play in my early twenties, but I didn't call myself a poet out loud in public, until I had served my apprenticeship to Milton's thankless muse

216

three times over. I wrote always in verse. In the medium of sound broadcasting I could shake off the trammels of blindness and deafness

It was thirty years later as I was crossing that wasteland on the last stages of my journey into darkness, I had my only experience of the dark night of the soul.

Moments bordering on despair, yes these I had had, fleetingly. Moments when I had said, to my pillow and my god: It is not fair. It is unjust.

For years I had had one of the greatest fights a poet could wish, fighting insomnia. This gift I had used as soon as I learned to stop worrying about it instead of blessing it for the boon it was.

At that most dangerous hour which comes before the dawn all the defences of my spirit crumbled. I knew that in a matter of months the shadows would close upon my sight.

What's the use of being a poet if one cannot call upon the centre of one's being in the hour of agony? Much frustrated by two barriers, I have loved what Lincoln called the common man. But only saints can love their fellows *all* the time. The common man had in his generosity taught me countless wonderful things. But I was a poet. I was at home with angels and archangels, and had talked with dead queens in the tomb. In my terrible sense of impending, inevitable loss, I thought of the light I was to lose. Light, soft as peach bloom, hard as brass, bright commonplace commonday. I thought, with horror, of night. And day came to me and spoke to me as I had spoken to dead queens.

"You," he said, "who commune with poets dead and gone, consider what Walter de la Mare told you when you were young. 'Look your last on all things lovely every passing hour.' You are not yet wholly blind. Go. When the sun has risen, throw yourself face downwards and look into the Forest of the Grass."

The sun pressed down my shoulders with a warm, compelling hand. Rays of sunlight stabbed down into the forest like blades of broken glass, the jagged black shadows of the myriad blades of the grass criss-crossing down to their roots. In the forest there were glades and woods and rides down which wolf-spiders hunted their prey, the aphides. Snail shells, huge, humbug-striped brown and white spiral boulders littered the open glades. From matted thickets cockchafers exploded upwards like rocketing pheasants. Crickets rasped their two-string fiddles, Pop groups sent crazy by their own monotonous rhythm. Columns of black and red and yellow ants deployed their marching ranks directed by military intelligences alien to man.

To the millions of mites and midges the sun must have seemed a green glare in a remote green sky far above the forest treetops. A field mouse, as huge in proportion as an elephant, rushed across a clearing and froze into terrified stillness as a shadow fell upon it.

The raking talons struck as the falcon braked its headlong stoop. The claws missed and the hawk was up and away. A stag beetle like a shiny black dragon butted its horns against the stem of a hemlock as large to the creature as an oak. What had been hunting it?

A strong, heady smell of meadowsweet drifted across my nostrils, a smell made heavier by the scent of hundreds of flowers blended with it. The patch of grass on which I lay made me feel, imaginatively, the size of a brontosaurus in a primitive swamp. And all these millions of earth's other children were obeying the jungle law: 'eat or be eaten', and playing out the endless humming, humdrum dramas of the hunters and the hunted close to my fading eyes.

Rising, crampedly, I brushed a clot of cuckoo-spit from my wrist. I had destroyed a miniature Xanadu, a pleasure dome of multi-faceted, cloudy glass. I could not find the tiny, lead-coloured creature who had made that rare device. A froghopper, perhaps a quarter of an inch in length and thinner than a fragment of graphite. It had stuck its minute proboscis into a grass stem, sucked in the sap and blown the bubble which was to conceal it from the pterodactil eyes and beak of a thrush or blackbird.

I knew that I would carry with me into the country of the blind sharp, clear visual memories of a sub-world few of the sighted ever see.

That night in my insomniac spell, I knew that the dark night of the soul had lifted its dreadful cloud and its dreadful cloud would return to me no more.

Day had given me treasure untold from the moment when my newly opened eyes had been dazzled, I did not know by light.

Night would bring me such frights. Night would take away that most precious gift, the gift of sight.

Yet in the country of the blind, the poets were with me to a poet. And lo! it was no hostile land. Homer had been there before me, long ago. Milton. Humbert Wolfe, who had Englished some fragments of the Greek Anthology, laughed at me from the shades.

"Listen," he said, "To Meleager:
Flower or girl, which do you sell, none knows, for each, rose-girl, is equally a rose . . .
You can endure blindness.
"Listen again:

Seven Greek cities fought for Homer dead,
through which the living Homer begged his bread."
That's all very well, I thought. I'm not going to beg
mine. I'm going to earn it. I'm a Yorkshireman. That's
to say, pig-headed. If I hadn't been a fool as well I
would have gone to Black as soon as I took in the warning
of the lovely, dangerous rainbows. As it was, when I did
go at last, he saved a good quarter of the sight of my left
eye. For the year or two the improvement lasted, then he
operated on my right and balanced the sight of both of
them, see-sawing and drilling holes in them for another
three or four years before he could do no more for me
to shield what was left of my vision.

With a white stick and a pinch or two of courage it
wasn't too bad getting around at first. At last I was
beaten, in the sense that I could not go anywhere on my
own. And back trooped my Job's comforters. Deafness
didn't help me not to listen to them and every now and
then they had their way with me. Bad temper. Resentment. Lashing out.

And memory floated back to me, bread I had cast
upon the waters many a year before. The only poem I
had ever made in my sleep and put down on paper while
the dream was still vivid.

I fought my way back into that dream, slowly, as
words fight to make their way into a poem.

The dream was one of walking by the side of a river
in the owl-light, bat-light, twilight. Back in that dream
I loitered through a water meadow in Masham. I heard
in the dream, a vixen bark from the wood across the
river. Then silence. A silence in which I knew the
nocturnal stirrings of the wind in the wood, the small
sounds of night creatures, must have been going on

below the level of my listening. In a dream within a dream I became aware of another presence in the water meadow. A presence gliding over the dew-chill grass. Something, someone that made me eerily afraid. Fear passing beyond itself nerved me to whisper: "Who are you?"

Remote, cold as interstellar space the answering voice said "Night."

And I was no longer by the waterside but in my bed and waking with a dream-poem transcendentally singing in my head. The singing stayed with me as I touch-typed the words.

Dusk, the old negro porter of the Palace of Sleep, has lost the keys of delight and terror. How often, how vainly have I paced the palace's courtyard, ashen as the asphodel, the hueless lillies of hell?

In the mirror of the lead fountain I count, count, count, count, count the moon's sheep in their fleeces of cloud-wrack silver. There is no shepherd to guard them as they leap over the hurdles of the fold of heaven. There is no shepherd. There is no shepherdess. The ears of my mind are pricked by a she-wolf's howling, as she circles, circles, prowling at midnight's noon the desolate splendour of the fields of the moon. A touch as light as the fall of a petal of asphodel brushed my shoulder, and the voice which whispered, made the air of the courtyard colder yet warmer than velvet, was the voice that murmured: I am Night.

The doors of the Palace of Sleep, the most splendid of all palaces, even such, flew open at her touch. So Night, the sorceress, led me to explore floor after floor of the tortuous rooms of terror, the rooms of delight up, up to the Whispering Gallery's fearful height. I do

221

not remember the music, but music drifted, in rhythms subtly changing second by second. Somewhere in the rooms of delight a curtain lifted and a white finger beckoned.

The voice of Night is a rustle through the summer corn.

When the winter sea, with hugely-heaving waves and foundering gulfs, overwhelms the land's defences its passionate voice is hers.

The beat of the wings of the wild geese flying a skeming across the autumn moon is the rhythm of her voice.

All nocturnal creatures who seek their mates in spring desire them with her voice.

All living things which have their hope and their fears by day make themselves known to my inward ear through her, for to me the day is as the dark.

And Night speaks to me, in dreaming and in waking, with all her velvet, all her violent voices.

Through all her voices now Night says to me:

"You feared me once more than you feared your maker. He who said: 'And god divided the light from the darkness, and god called the light day, and the darkness he called night.'

"You shall fear me no longer.

"I will be with you always, more loyal than any friend, more faithful than a wife, closer to you than a lover.

"You who are blind, I will unseal your eyes and make you see.

"To be a poet is to be a seer.

"Call on your poets. Call on Omar, the Persian who saw but failed to fathom what he saw."

And Khayyam, Englished by Fitzgerald, said:

Then to rolling heaven itself I cried,

222

asking: What lamp had destiny to guide
her little children stumbling in the dark.
And: A blind understanding, heaven replied.
What Omar understood and gloried in was life. And
gloriously he sang of it.

Give me a book of verse beneath the bough,
a loaf of bread, a flask of wine and Thou
beside me singing in the wilderness
and wilderness were paradise enow.

A courtier, a mathematician he loved to use his mind.

Up from earth's centre through the seventh gate
I rose and on the throne of Saturn sate
and many knots unravelled by the way but not the
knot of human life and fate.

But a deep sadness overcast his mind:

Oh, thou who didst with pitfall and with gin
beset the path I was to wander in,
thou wilt not with predestination fond
enmesh me and impute my fall to sin?

I heard him singing through Fitzgerald's voice. I heard
God laughing through the voice of night.

Night, with me always, closer to me than a lover,
has kept her word. She has unsealed my eyes.

The dark tower of my blindness overflows with light.

Black, chaotic, yet Night has shown me worlds, stars,
suns, eyes bright as Blake's tyger, all diverse: but single
is light.

One, whether burning in mines of candles before the
high altar or blazing and shaking harsh, hard and metallic
as it bursts from the atom bomb, burns, like all flame,
to Gods glory: light Christ of love, sight.

It is most good to know that although I cannot
physically see the splendour of island universes they are
there.

As it is good to know that my lilac tree is there and will bloom again in a spring I cannot see but can intensely apprehend.

I have travelled for seventy years through this world. I set out in light and could not see my way, for at first that way seemed to me to lead through the wasteland of frustration and disappointment.

Journeying, I found it was a flowering wilderness.

I journeyed on, through deepening shadows, to the edge of darkness.

The valley of the shadow of death cannot be far ahead. I hope I shall walk through it the more resolute for being used to shadows.

If I falter and stumble when I sense that the deepest of all shadows are about me, what does it matter? Mine eyes, as King Lear said, are none of the best.

Lord, I believe.

Help thou mine unbelief.

I believe that at the end of the valley

I shall come to the edge of light.

The light which will destroy my blind misunderstanding by showing me who I am: nothing, until being is drawn into the light of the incomprehensible love of God.